Sweet Escapes

A Journey Through Divine Desserts and Pies

By

Kelly N. Knowles

FROSTING OR ICING.

In the first place, the eggs should be cold, and the platter on which they are to be beaten also cold. Allow, for the white of one egg, one small teacupful of powdered sugar. Break the eggs and throw a small handful of the sugar on them as soon as you begin beating; keep adding it at intervals until it is all used up. The eggs must *not* be beaten until the sugar has been added in this way, which gives a smooth, tender frosting, and one that will dry much sooner than the old way.

Spread with a broad knife evenly over the cake, and if it seems too thin, beat in a little more sugar. Cover the cake with two coats, the second after the first has become dry, or nearly so. If the icing gets too dry or stiff before the last coat is needed, it can be thinned sufficiently with a little water, enough to make it work smoothly.

A little lemon juice, or half a teaspoonful of tartaric acid, added to the frosting while being beaten, makes it white and more frothy.

The flavors mostly used are lemon, vanilla, almond, rose, chocolate and orange. If you wish to ornament with figures or flowers, make up rather more icing, keep about one-third out until that on the cake is dried; then, with a clean glass syringe, apply it in such forms as you desire and dry as before; what you keep out to ornament with may be tinted pink with cochineal, blue with indigo, yellow with saffron or the grated rind of an orange strained through a cloth, green with spinach juice and brown with chocolate, purple with cochineal and indigo. Strawberry, or currant and cranberry juices color a delicate pink.

Set the cake in a cool oven with the door open to dry, or in a draught in an open window.

ALMOND FROSTING.

The whites of three eggs, beaten up with three cups of fine, white sugar. Blanch a pound of sweet almonds, pound them in a mortar with a little sugar, until a fine paste, then add the whites of eggs, sugar and vanilla extract. Pound a few minutes to thoroughly mix. Cover the cake with a very thick coating of this, set in a cool oven to dry, afterwards cover with a plain icing.

CHOCOLATE FROSTING.

The whites of four eggs, three cups of powdered sugar and nearly a cup of grated chocolate. Beat the whites a very little, they must not become white, stir in the chocolate, then put in the sugar gradually, beating to mix it well.

PLAIN CHOCOLATE ICING.

Put into a shallow pan four tablespoonfuls of scraped chocolate, and place it where it will melt gradually, but not scorch; when melted, stir in three tablespoonfuls of milk or cream and one of water; mix all well together, and add one scant teacupful of sugar; boil about five minutes, and while hot, and when the cakes are nearly cold, spread some evenly over the surface of one of the cakes; put a second one on top, alternating the mixture and cakes; then cover top and sides, and set in a warm oven to harden. All who have tried recipe after recipe, vainly hoping to find one where the chocolate sticks to the cake and not to the fingers, will appreciate the above. In making those most palatable of cakes, "Chocolate Eclairs," the recipe just given will be found very satisfactory.

TUTTI FRUTTI ICING.

Mix with boiled icing one ounce each of chopped citron, candied cherries, seedless raisins, candied pineapple and blanched almonds.

SUGAR ICING.

To one pound of extra refined sugar add one ounce of fine white starch; pound finely together and then sift them through gauze; then beat the whites of three eggs to a froth. The secret of success is to beat the eggs long enough, and always one way; add the powdered sugar by degrees, or it will spoil the froth of the eggs. When all the sugar is stirred in continue the whipping for half an hour longer, adding more sugar if the ice is too thin. Take a little of the icing and lay it aside for ornamenting afterward. When the cake comes out of the oven, spread the sugar icing smoothly over it with a knife and dry it at once in a cool oven. For ornamenting the cake the icing may be tinged any color preferred. For pink, use a few drops of cochineal; for yellow, a pinch of saffron dissolved; for green, the juice of some chopped spinach. Whichever is chosen, let the coloring be first mixed with a little colorless spirit and then stirred into the white icing until the tint is deep enough. To ornament the cake with it, make a cone of stiff writing paper and squeeze the colored icing through it, so as to form leaves, beading or letters, as the case may be. It requires nicety and care to do it with success.

BOILED FROSTING.

To one pound of finest pulverized sugar add three wine-glassfuls of clear water. Let it stand until it dissolves; then boil it until it is perfectly clear and threads from the spoon. Beat well the whites of four eggs. Pour the sugar into the dish with the eggs, but do not mix them until the syrup is luke-warm; then beat all well together for one-half hour.

Season to your taste with vanilla, rose-water, or lemon juice. The first coating may be put on the cake as soon as it is well mixed. Rub the cake with a little flour before you apply the icing. While the first coat is drying continue to beat the remainder; you will not have to wait long if the cake is set in a warm place near the fire. This is said to be a most excellent recipe for icing.

FROSTING WITHOUT EGGS.

An excellent frosting may be made without eggs or gelatine, which will keep longer and cut more easily, causing no breakage or crumbling and withal is very economical.

Take one cup of granulated sugar; dampen it with one-fourth of a cup of milk, or five tablespoonfuls; place it on the fire in a suitable dish and stir it until it boils; then let it boil for five minutes without stirring; remove it from the fire and set the dish in another of cold water; add flavoring. While it is cooling, stir or beat it constantly and it will become a thick, creamy frosting.

GELATINE FROSTING.

Soak one teaspoonful of gelatine in one tablespoonful of cold water half an hour, dissolve in two tablespoonfuls of hot water; add one cup of powdered sugar and stir until smooth.

GOLDEN FROSTING.

A very delicious and handsome frosting can be made by using the yolks of eggs instead of the whites. Proceed exactly as for ordinary frosting. It will harden just as nicely as that does. This is particularly good for orange cake, harmonizing with the color of the cake in a way to please those who love rich coloring.

FILLINGS FOR LAYER CAKES.

No. 1. CREAM FILLING.

Cream filling is made with one pint of new milk, two eggs, three tablespoonfuls of sifted flour (or half cup of cornstarch), one cup of sugar. Put two-thirds of the milk on the stove to boil, stir the sugar, flour and eggs in what is left. When the milk boils, put into it the whole and cook it until it is as thick as custard; when cool, add vanilla extract. This custard is nice with a cup of hickory nuts, kernels chopped fine and stirred into it. Spread between the layers of cake. This custard can be made of the yolks of the eggs only, saving the whites for the cake part.

No. 2. ANOTHER CREAM FILLING.

One cup powdered sugar, one-fourth cup hot water. Let them simmer. Beat white of an egg and mix with the above; when cold, add one-half cup chopped raisins, one-half cup chopped walnuts, one tablespoonful of grated cocoanut.

No. 3. ICE-CREAM FILLING.

Make an icing as follows: Three cups of sugar, one of water; boil to a thick, clear syrup, or until it begins to be brittle; pour this, boiling hot, over the *well-beaten* whites of three eggs; stir the mixture very briskly, and pour the sugar in slowly; beat it, when all in, until cool. Flavor with lemon or vanilla extract. This, spread between any white cake layers, answers for "Ice-Cream Cake."

No. 4. APPLE FILLING.

Peel and slice green tart apples, put them on the fire with sugar to suit; when tender, remove, rub them through a fine sieve and add a small piece of butter. When cold, use to spread between the layers; cover the cake with plenty of sugar.

No. 5. ANOTHER APPLE FILLING.

One coffeecup of sugar, one egg, three large apples grated, one lemon grated, juice and outside of the rind; beat together and cook till quite thick. To be cooled before putting on the cake. Spread between layers of cake.

No. 6. CREAM FROSTING.

A cup of sweet thick cream whipped, sweetened and flavored with vanilla; cut a loaf of cake in two, spread the frosting between and on the top; this tastes like Charlotte Russe.

No. 7. PEACH-CREAM FILLING.

Cut peaches into thin slices, or chop them and prepare cream by whipping and sweetening. Put a layer of peaches between the layers of cake and pour cream over each layer and over the top. Bananas, strawberries or other fruits may be used in the same way, mashing strawberries and stewing thick with powdered sugar.

No. 8. CHOCOLATE CREAM FOR FILLING.

Five tablespoonfuls of grated chocolate, enough cream or milk to wet it, one cupful of sugar, one egg, one teaspoonful vanilla flavoring. Stir the ingredients over the fire until thoroughly mixed, having beaten the egg well before adding it; then add the vanilla flavoring after it is removed from the fire.

No. 9. ANOTHER CHOCOLATE FILLING.

The whites of three eggs beaten stiff, one cup of sugar and one cup of grated chocolate, put between the layers and on top.

No. 10. BANANA FILLING.

Make an icing of the whites of two eggs and one cup and a half of powdered sugar. Spread this on the layers, and then cover thickly and entirely with bananas sliced thin or chopped fine. This cake may be flavored with vanilla. The top should be simply frosted.

No. 11. LEMON JELLY FILLING.

Grate the yellow from the rind of two lemons and squeeze out the juice; two cupfuls of sugar, the yolks and whites of two eggs beaten separately. Mix the sugar and yolks, then add the whites and then the lemons. Now pour on a cupful of boiling water; stir into this two tablespoonfuls of sifted flour, rubbed smooth in half a cup of water; then add a tablespoonful of melted butter; cook until it thickens. When cold, spread between the layers of cake. Oranges can be used in place of lemons.

Another filling of lemon (without cooking) is made of the grated rind and juice of two lemons and the whites of two eggs beaten with one cup of sugar.

No. 12. ORANGE CAKE FILLING.

Peel two large oranges, remove the seeds, chop them fine, add half a peeled lemon, one cup of sugar and the well-beaten white of an egg. Spread between the layers of "Silver Cake" recipe.

No. 13. FIG FILLING.

Take a pound of figs, chop fine, and put into a stewpan on the stove; pour over them a teacupful of water and add a half cup of sugar. Cook all together until soft and smooth. When cold spread between layers of cake.

No. 14. FRUIT FILLING.

Four tablespoonfuls of *very finely* chopped citron, four tablespoonfuls of finely chopped seeded raisins, half a cupful of blanched almonds chopped fine, also a quarter of a pound of finely chopped figs. Beat the whites of three eggs to a stiff froth, adding half of a cupful of sugar; then mix thoroughly into this the whole of the chopped ingredients. Put it between the layers of cake when the cake is *hot*, so that it will cook the egg a little. This will be found delicious.

BREAD OR RAISED CAKE.

Two cupfuls of raised dough; beat into it two-thirds of a cup of butter and two cups of sugar creamed together, three eggs, well beaten, one even teaspoonful of soda dissolved in two tablespoonfuls of milk, half a nutmeg grated, one tablespoonful of cinnamon, a teaspoonful of cloves, one cup of raisins. Mix all well together, put in the beaten whites of eggs and raisins last; beat all hard for several minutes; put in buttered pans and let it stand half an hour to rise again before baking. Bake in a *moderate* oven. Half a glass of brandy is an improvement, if you have it convenient.

FRUIT CAKE. (Superior.)

Three pounds dry flour, one pound sweet butter, one pound sugar, three pounds stoned raisins, two pounds currants, three-quarters of a pound sweet almonds blanched, one pound citron, twelve eggs, one tablespoonful allspice, one teaspoonful cloves, two tablespoonfuls cinnamon, two nutmegs, one wine-glass of wine, one wine-glass of brandy, one coffeecupful molasses with the spices in it; steep this gently twenty or thirty minutes, not boiling hot; beat the eggs very lightly; put the fruit in last, stirring it gradually, also a teaspoonful of soda dissolved in a tablespoonful of water; the fruit should be well floured; if necessary add flour after the fruit is in; butter a sheet of paper and lay it in the pan. Lay in some slices of citron, then a layer of the mixture, then of citron again, etc., till the pan is nearly full. Bake three or four hours, according to the thickness of the loaves, in a tolerably hot oven, and with steady heat. Let it cool in the oven gradually. Ice when cold. It improves this cake very much to add three teaspoonfuls of baking powder to the flour. A fine wedding cake recipe.

FRUIT CAKE BY MEASURE, (Excellent.)

Two scant teacupfuls of butter, three cupfuls of dark brown sugar, six eggs, whites and yolks beaten separately, one pound of raisins, seeded, one of currants, washed and dried, and half a pound of citron cut in thin strips; also half a cupful of cooking molasses and half a cupful of sour milk. Stir the butter and sugar to a cream, add to that half a grated nutmeg, ope tablespoonful of ground cinnamon, one teaspoonful of cloves, one teaspoonful of mace, add the molasses and sour milk. Stir all well; then put in the beaten yolks of eggs, a wine-glass of brandy; stir again all thoroughly, and then add four cupfuls of sifted flour alternately with the beaten whites of eggs. Now dissolve a level teaspoonful of soda and stir in thoroughly. Mix the fruit together and stir into it two heaping tablespoonfuls of flour; then stir it in the cake. Butter two common-sized baking tins carefully, line them with letter paper well buttered, and bake in a moderate oven two hours. After it is baked, let it cool in the pan. Afterward put it into a tight can, or let it remain in the pans and cover tightly. Best recipe of all.

Mrs. S. A. Camp, Grand Rapids, Mich.

WHITE FRUIT CAKE.

One cup of butter, two cups of sugar, one cup of sweet milk, two and one-half cups of flour, the whites of seven eggs, two even teaspoonfuls of baking powder, one pound each of seeded raisins, figs and blanched almonds, and one quarter of a pound of citron, all chopped fine. Mix all thoroughly before adding the fruit; add a teaspoonful of lemon extract. Put baking powder in the flour and mix it well before adding it to the other ingredients. Sift a little flour over the fruit before stirring it in. Bake slowly two hours and try with a splint to see when it is done. A cup of grated cocoanut is a nice addition to this cake.

MOLASSES FRUIT CAKE.

One teacupful of butter, one teacupful of brown sugar, worked well together; next, two teacupfuls of cooking molasses, one cupful of milk with a teaspoonful of soda dissolved in it, one tablespoonful of ginger, one tablespoonful of cinnamon and one teaspoonful of cloves a little grated nutmeg. Now add four eggs well beaten and five cups of sifted flour, or enough to make a stiff batter. Flour a cup of raisins and one of currants; add last. Bake in a very *moderate* oven one hour. If well covered will keep six months.

SPONGE CAKE.

SEPARATE the whites and yolks of six eggs. Beat the yolks to a cream, to which add two teacupfuls of powdered sugar, beating again from five to ten minutes, then add two tablespoonfuls of milk or water, a pinch of salt and flavoring. Now add part of the beaten whites; then two cups of flour in which you have sifted two teaspoonfuls of baking powder; mix gradually into the above ingredients, stirring slowly and lightly, only enough to mix them well; lastly add the remainder of the whites of the eggs. Line the tins with buttered paper and fill two-thirds full.

WHITE SPONGE CAKE.

Whites of five eggs, one cup of flour, one cup sugar, one teaspoonful baking powder; flavor with vanilla. Bake in a quick oven.

ALMOND SPONGE CAKE.

The addition of almonds makes this cake very superior to the usual sponge cake. Sift one pint of fine flour; blanch in scalding water two ounces of sweet and two ounces of bitter almonds, renewing the hot water when expedient; when the skins are all off wash the almonds in cold water (mixing the sweet and bitter) and wipe them dry; pound them to a fine, smooth paste (one at a time), adding, as you proceed, water or white of egg to prevent their boiling. Set them in a cool place; beat ten eggs, the whites and yolks separately, till very smooth and thick, and then beat into them gradually two cups powdered sugar in turn with the pounded almonds; lastly, add the flour, stirring it round slowly and lightly on the surface of the mixture, as in common sponge cake; have ready buttered a *deep* square pan; put the mixture carefully into it, set into the oven and bake till thoroughly done and risen very high; when cool, cover it with plain white icing flavored with rose-water, or with almond icing. With sweet almonds always use a small portion of bitter; without them, *sweet* almonds have little or no taste, though they add to the richness of the cake.

Use two heaping teaspoonfuls of baking powder in the flour.

OLD-FASHIONED SPONGE CAKE.

Two cups of sifted white sugar, two cups of flour measured before sifting, ten eggs. Stir the yolks and sugar together until perfectly light; add a pinch of salt; beat the whites of the eggs to a very stiff froth and add them with the flour, after beating together lightly; flavor with lemon. Bake in a *moderate* oven about forty-five minutes. Baking powder is an improvement to this cake, using two large teaspoonfuls.

LEMON SPONGE CAKE.

Into one level cup of flour put a level teaspoonful of baking powder and sift it. Grate off the yellow rind of a lemon. Separate the whites from the yolks of four eggs. Measure a scant cup of white granulated sugar and beat it to a cream with the yolks, then add the grated rind and a tablespoonful of the juice of the lemon. Stir together until thick and creamy; now beat the whites to a stiff froth; then quickly and lightly mix *without beating* a third of the flour with the yolks; then a third of the whites; then more flour and whites until all are used. The mode of mixing must be very light, rather cutting down through the cake batter than to beating it; beating the eggs makes them light, but beating the batter makes the cake tough. Bake immediately until a straw run into it can be withdrawn clean.

This recipe is especially nice for Charlotte Russe, being so light and porous.

PLAIN SPONGE CAKE.

Beat the yolks of four eggs together with two cups of fine powdered sugar. Stir in gradually one cup of sifted flour and the whites of four eggs beaten to a stiff froth, then a cup of sifted flour in which two teaspoonfuls of baking powder have been stirred, and, lastly, a scant teacupful of boiling water, stirred in a little at a time. Flavor, add salt and, however thin the mixture may seem, do not add any more flour. Bake in shallow tins.

BRIDE'S CAKE.

Cream together one scant cup of butter and three cups of sugar; add one cup of milk, then the beaten whites of twelve eggs; sift three teaspoonfuls of baking powder into one cup of cornstarch mixed with three cups of sifted flour and beat in gradually with the rest; flavor to taste. Beat all thoroughly, then put in buttered tins lined with letter paper well buttered; bake slowly in a *moderate* oven. A beautiful white cake. Ice the top. Double the recipe if more is required.

ENGLISH POUND CAKE.

One pound of butter, one and one-quarter pounds of flour, one pound of pounded loaf sugar, one pound of currants, nine eggs, two ounces of candied peel, one-half ounce of citron, one-half ounce of sweet almonds; when liked, a little pounded mace. Work the butter to a cream; add the sugar, then the well-beaten yolks of eggs, next the flour, currants, candied peel, which should be cut into neat slices, and the almonds, which should be blanched and chopped, and mix all these well together; whisk the whites of eggs and let them be thoroughly blended with the other ingredients. Beat the cake well for twenty minutes and put it into a round tin, lined at the bottom and sides with strips of white buttered paper. Bake it from two hours to two and a half, and let the oven be well heated when the cake is first put in, as, if this is not the case, the currants will all sink to the bottom of it. A glass of wine is usually added to the mixture, but this is scarcely necessary, as the cake will be found quite rich enough without it.

PLAIN POUND CAKE.

This is the old-fashioned recipe that our mothers used to make, and it can be kept for weeks in an earthen jar, closely covered, first dipping letter paper in brandy and placing over the top of the cake before covering the jar.

Beat to a cream one pound of butter with one pound of sugar, after mixing well with the beaten yolks of twelve eggs, one grated nutmeg, one glass of wine, one glass of rose-water. Then stir in one pound of sifted flour and the well-beaten whites of the eggs. Bake a nice light brown.

COCOANUT POUND CAKE.

One-half cupful of butter, two cupfuls of sugar, one cupful of milk, and five eggs, beaten to a stiff froth; one teaspoonful of soda and two of cream of tartar, stirred into four cups of sifted flour. Beat the butter and sugar until very light; to which add the beaten yolks, then the milk, the beaten whites of eggs, then the flour by degrees. After beating all well together, add a small cocoanut grated. Line the cake-pans with paper well buttered, fill rather more than half full and bake in a *moderate* oven. Spread over the top a thin frosting, sprinkled thickly with grated cocoanut.

CITRON POUND CAKE.

Stir two cups of butter to a cream, then beat in the following ingredients each one in succession: one pint of powdered sugar, one quart of flour, a teaspoonful of salt; eight eggs, the yolks and whites beaten separately, and a wine-glass of brandy; then last of all add a quarter of a pound of citron cut into thin slices and floured. Line two cake pans with buttered paper and turn the cake batter in. Bake in a *moderate* oven about three-quarters of an hour.

CITRON CAKE.

Three cups of white sugar and one cup of butter creamed together; one cup of sweet milk, six eggs, whites and yolks beaten separately, one teaspoonful of vanilla or lemon extract, two heaping teaspoonfuls of baking powder, sifted with four cups and a half of flour. One cup and a half of citron, sliced thin and dredged with flour. Divide into two cakes and bake in tins lined with buttered letter paper.

LEMON CAKE.

Three teacupfuls of sugar, one cupful of butter, five eggs, a level teaspoonful of soda dissolved in a cup of sweet milk, four full cups of sifted flour and lastly the grated peel and juice of a lemon, the juice to be added the very last. Bake in two shallow tins. When cold ice with lemon icing and cut into squares.

DELICATE CAKE.

One cup of cornstarch, one of butter, two of sugar, one of sweet milk, two of flour, the whites of seven eggs; rub butter and sugar to a cream; mix one teaspoonful cream of tartar with the flour and cornstarch; one-half teaspoonful soda with the sweet milk; add the milk and soda to the sugar and butter, then add flour, then the whites of eggs; flavor to taste. Never fails to be good.

SILVER, OR DELICATE CAKE.

Whites of six eggs, one cupful of sweet milk, two cupfuls of sugar, four cupfuls of sifted flour, two-thirds of a cup of butter, flavoring and two teaspoonfuls of baking powder. Stir the sugar and butter to a cream, then add the milk and flavoring, part of the flour, the beaten whites of eggs, then the rest of the flour. Bake carefully in tins lined with buttered white paper.

When using the whites of eggs for nice cakes, the yolks need not be wasted; keep them in a cool place and scramble them. Serve on toast or with chipped beef.

GOLD CAKE.

After beating to a cream one cup and a half of butter and two cups of white sugar, stir in the well-whipped yolks of one dozen eggs, four cupfuls of sifted flour, one teaspoonful of baking powder. Flavor with lemon. Line the bake-pans with buttered paper and bake in a moderate oven for one hour.

GOLD OR LEMON CAKE.

Two cups of sugar, half a cup of butter, the yolks of six eggs and one whole one, the grated rind and juice of a lemon or orange, half a teaspoonful of soda dissolved in half a cup of sweet milk, four cups of sifted flour, sifted twice; cream the butter and sugar, then add the beaten yolks and the flour, beating hard for several minutes. Lastly, add the lemon or orange and bake, frosting if liked. This makes a more suitable *lemon* cake than if made with the white parts of eggs added.

SNOW CAKE. (Delicious.)

One pound of arrowroot, quarter of a pound of pounded white sugar, half a pound of butter, the whites of six eggs, flavoring to taste of essence of almonds, or vanilla, or lemon; beat the butter to a cream; stir in the sugar and arrowroot gradually, at the same time beating the mixture; whisk the whites of the eggs to a stiff froth; add them to the other ingredients and beat well for twenty minutes; put in which-ever of the above flavorings may be preferred; pour the cake into a buttered mold or tin and bake it in a *moderate* oven from one to one and a half hours.

This is a genuine Scotch recipe.

MARBLE CAKE.

White Part.—Whites of four eggs, one cup of white sugar, half a cup of butter, half a cup of sweet milk, two teaspoonfuls of baking powder, one teaspoonful of vanilla or lemon and two and a half cups of sifted flour.

Dark Part.—Yolks of four eggs, one cup of brown sugar, half a cup of cooking molasses, half a cup of butter, half a cup of sour milk, one teaspoonful of ground cloves, one teaspoonful of cinnamon, one teaspoonful of mace, one nutmeg grated, one teaspoonful of soda, the soda to be dissolved in a little milk and added after part of the flour is stirred in, one and a half cups of sifted flour.

Drop a spoonful of each kind in a well-buttered cake-dish, first the light part, then the dark, alternately. Try to drop it so that the cake shall be well-streaked through, so that it has the appearance of marble.

SUPERIOR LOAF CAKE.

Two cups of butter, three cups of sugar, two small cups of milk, seven cups of sifted flour; four eggs, the whites and yolks separately beaten; one teacupful of seeded raisins, one teacupful of well-washed and dried currants, one teacupful of sliced citron, one tablespoonful of powdered cinnamon, one teaspoonful of mace, one teaspoonful of soda and one teacupful of home-made yeast.

Take part of the butter and warm it with the milk; stir in part of the flour and the yeast and let it rise; then add the other ingredients with a wine-glass of wine or brandy. Turn all into well-buttered cake-tins and let rise again. Bake slowly in a *moderate* oven for two hours.

FRENCH CHOCOLATE CAKE.

The whites of seven eggs, two cups of sugar, two-thirds of a cup of butter, one cup of milk and three of flour and three teaspoonfuls of baking powder. The chocolate part of the cake is made just the same, only use the yolks of the eggs with a cup of grated chocolate stirred into it. Bake it in layers—the layers being light and dark; then spread a custard between them, which is made with two eggs, one pint of milk, one-half cup of sugar, one tablespoonful of flour or cornstarch; when cool flavor with vanilla, two teaspoonfuls. Fine.

CHOCOLATE CAKE. No. 1.

One cup of butter and two cups of sugar stirred to a cream, with the yolks of five eggs added after they have been well beaten. Then stir into that one cup of milk, beat the whites of two pf the eggs to a stiff froth and add that also; now put in three cups and a half of sifted flour, two heaping teaspoonfuls of baking powder having been stirred into it. Bake in jelly-cake tins.

Mixture for Filling.—Take the remaining three whites of the eggs beaten *very* stiff, two cupfuls of sugar boiled to almost candy or until it becomes stringy or almost brittle; take it hot from the fire and pour it very slowly on the beaten whites of egg, beating quite fast; add one-half cake of grated chocolate, a teaspoonful of vanilla extract. Stir it all until cool, then spread between each cake and over the top and sides. This, when well made, is the *premium* cake of its kind.

CHOCOLATE CAKE. No. 2.

One-half cup butter, two cups sugar, three-quarters of a cup sweet milk, two and one-half cups flour, whites of eight eggs, one teaspoonful of cream of tartar, one-half teaspoonful soda; bake in shallow pans.

For the Frosting.—Take the whites of three eggs, three tablespoonfuls of sugar and one tablespoonful of grated chocolate (confectioners') to one egg; put the cake together with the frosting, then frost the top of the cake with the same.

CHOCOLATE CAKE. No. 3.

Two cups sugar, one cup butter, yolks of five eggs and whites of two and one cup milk. Thoroughly mix two teaspoonfuls baking powder with three and one-half cups flour while dry; then mix all together. Bake in jelly tins.

Mixture for Filling.—Whites of three eggs, one and one-half cups of sugar, three tablespoonfuls of grated chocolate, one teaspoonful of vanilla. Beat together and spread between the layers and on top of the cake.

COCOANUT CAKE.

Cream together three-quarters of a cup of butter and two of white sugar; then add one cup of sweet milk, four eggs, whites and yolks separately beaten, the yolks added first to the butter and sugar, then the whites; flavor with lemon or vanilla; mix three heaping teaspoonfuls of baking powder in three cups of sifted flour and add last; bake in jelly pans.

For Filling.—Make an icing by beating the whites of three eggs and a cup of powdered sugar to a stiff froth. When the cake is cooled, spread a thick layer of this frosting over each cake, and sprinkle very thickly with grated cocoanut.

COCOANUT AND ALMOND CAKE.

Two and one-half cups powdered sugar, one cup butter, four full cups prepared flour, whites of seven eggs whisked stiff, one small cup of milk, with a mere pinch of soda, one grated cocoanut, one-half teaspoonful nutmeg, the juice and half the grated peel of one lemon; cream butter and sugar; stir in lemon and nutmeg; mix well; add the milk and whites and flour alternately. Lastly, stir in the grated cocoanut swiftly and lightly. Bake in four jelly-cake tins.

Filling.—One pound sweet almonds, whites of four eggs whisked stiff, one heaping cup powdered sugar, two teaspoonfuls rose-water. Blanch the almonds. Let them get cold and dry; then pound in a Wedgewood mortar, adding rose-water as you go. Save about two dozen to shred for the top. Stir the paste into the icing after it is made; spread between the cooled cakes; make that for the top a trifle thicker and lay it on heavily. When it has stiffened somewhat, stick the shred almonds closely over it. Set in the oven to harden, but do not let it scorch.

COFFEE CAKE.

One cup of brown sugar, one cup of butter, two eggs, one-half cup of molasses, one cup of strong, cold coffee, one teaspoonful of soda, two teaspoonfuls of cinnamon, one teaspoonful of cloves, one cup of raisins or currants and five cups of sifted flour. Add the fruit last, rubbed in a little of the flour. Bake about one hour.

FEATHER CAKE.

One egg, one cup of sugar, one tablespoonful of cold butter, half a cup of milk, one and one-half cups of flour, one teaspoonful of cream of tartar, half a teaspoonful of soda. A nice plain cake—to be eaten while it is fresh. A spoonful of dried apple sauce or of peach sauce, a spoonful of jelly, the same of lemon extract, nutmeg, cinnamon, cloves and spice—ground—or half a cupful of raisins might be added for a change.

ELECTION CAKE.

Three cups milk, two cups sugar, one cup yeast; stir to a batter and let stand over night; in the morning add two cups sugar, two cups butter, three eggs, half a nutmeg, one tablespoonful cinnamon, one pound raisins, a gill of brandy.

Brown sugar is much better than white for this kind of cake, and it is improved by dissolving a half-teaspoonful of soda in a tablespoonful of milk in the morning. It should stand in the greased pans and rise some time until quite light before baking.

CREAM CAKE.

Four eggs, whites and yolks beaten separately, two teacups of sugar, one cup of sweet cream, two heaping cupfuls of flour, one teaspoonful of soda, mix two teaspoonfuls of cream of tartar in the flour before sifting. Add the whites the last thing before the flour and stir that in gently without beating.

GOLDEN CREAM CAKE.

Yolks of eight eggs beaten to the lightest possible cream, two cupfuls of sugar, a pinch of salt, three teaspoonfuls of baking powder sifted well with flour. Bake in three jelly-cake pans. Make an icing of the whites of three eggs and one pound of sugar. Spread it between the cakes and sprinkle grated cocoanut thickly over each layer. It is delicious when properly made.

DRIED APPLE FRUIT CAKE.

Soak three cupfuls of dried apples over night in cold water enough to swell them; chop them in the morning and put them on the fire with three cups of molasses; stew until almost soft; add a cupful of nice raisins (seedless, if possible) and stew a few moments; when cold, add three cupfuls of flour, one cupful of butter, three eggs and a teaspoonful of soda; bake in a steady oven. This will make two good-sized panfuls of splendid cake; the apples will cook like citron and taste deliciously. Raisins may be omitted; also spices to taste may be added. This is not a dear but a delicious cake.

CAKE WITHOUT EGGS.

Beat together one teacupful of butter and three teacupfuls of sugar, and when quite light stir in one pint of sifted flour. Add to this one pound of raisins seeded and chopped, then mixed with a cup of sifted flour one-teaspoonful of nutmeg, one teaspoonful of powdered cinnamon and lastly one pint of thick sour cream or milk in which a teaspoonful of soda is dissolved. Bake immediately in buttered tins one hour in a *moderate* oven.

WHITE MOUNTAIN CAKE No. 1.

Two cups of sugar, two-thirds cup of butter, the whites of seven eggs well beaten, two-thirds cup of sweet milk, two cups of flour, one cup of cornstarch, two teaspoonfuls baking powder. Bake in jelly-cake tins.

Frosting.—Whites of three eggs and some sugar beaten together not quite as stiff as usual for frosting; spread over the cake, add some grated cocoanut, then put your cakes together; put cocoanut and frosting on top.

WHITE MOUNTAIN CAKE. No. 2.

Cream three cupfuls of sugar and one of butter, making it very light, then add a cupful of milk. Beat the whites of eight eggs very stiff, add half of those to the other ingredients. Mix well into four cups of sifted flour one tablespoonful of baking powder; stir this into the cake, add flavoring, then the remaining beaten whites of egg. Bake in layers like jelly cake. Make an icing for the filling, using the whites of four eggs beaten to a very stiff froth, with two cups of fine white sugar and the juice of half a lemon. Spread each layer of the cake thickly with this icing, place one on another, then ice all over the top and sides. The yolks left from this cake may be used to make a spice cake from the recipe of "Golden Spice Cake."

QUEEN'S CAKE.

Beat well together one cupful of butter and three cupfuls of white sugar, add the yolks of six eggs and one cupful of milk, two teaspoonfuls of vanilla or lemon extract. Mix all thoroughly. To four cupfuls of flour add two heaping teaspoonfuls of cream of tartar and sift gently over the cake stirring all the time. To this add one even teaspoonful of soda dissolved in one tablespoonful of warm water. Mix it well. Stir in gently the whites of six eggs beaten to a stiff foam. Bake slowly. It should be put in the oven as soon as possible after putting in the soda and whites of eggs.

This is the same recipe as the one for "Citron Cake," only omitting the citron.

ANGEL CAKE.

Put into one tumbler of flour one teaspoonful of cream of tartar, then sift it five times. Sift also one glass and a half of white powdered sugar. Beat to a stiff froth the whites of eleven eggs; stir the sugar into the eggs by degrees, very lightly and carefully, adding three teaspoonfuls of vanilla extract. After this add the flour, stirring quickly and lightly. Pour it into a clean, bright tin cake-dish, which should *not* be buttered or lined. Bake at once in a moderate oven about forty minutes, testing it with a broom splint. When done let it remain in the cake-tin, turning it upside down, with the sides resting on the tops of two saucers so that a current of air will pass under and over it.

This is the best recipe found after trying several. A perfection cake.

WASHINGTON LOAF CAKE.

Three cups of sugar, two scant cups of butter, one cup of sour milk, five eggs and one teaspoonful of soda, three tablespoonfuls of cinnamon, half a nutmeg grated and two cups of raisins, one of currants and four cups of sifted flour.

Mix as usual and stir the fruit in at the last, dredged in flour. Line the cake-pans with paper well buttered. This cake will take longer to bake than plain; the heat of the oven must be kept at an even temperature.

MAKING THE PIES.

MAKING THE PIES.

RIBBON CAKE.

This cake is made from the same recipe as marble cake, only make double the quantity of the white part, and divide it in one-half; put into it a very little cochineal. It will be a delicate pink. Bake in jelly-cake tins and lay first the white, then the dark, then the pink one on top of the others; put together with frosting between. It makes quite a fancy cake. Frost the top when cool.

GOLDEN SPICE CAKE.

This cake can be made to advantage when you have the yolks of eggs left, after having used the whites in making white cake. Take the yolks of seven eggs and one whole egg, two cupfuls of brown sugar, one cupful of molasses, one cupful of butter, one large coffeecupful of sour milk, one teaspoonful of soda (just even full) and five cupfuls of flour, one teaspoonful of ground cloves, two teaspoonfuls of cinnamon, two teaspoonfuls of ginger, one nutmeg and a small pinch of cayenne pepper; beat eggs, sugar and butter to a light batter before putting in the molasses, then add the molasses, flour and milk; beat it well together and bake in a *moderate* oven; if fruit is used, take two cupfuls of raisins, flour them well and put them in last.

ALMOND CAKE.

One-half cupful butter, two cupfuls sugar, four eggs, one-half cupful almonds, blanched—by pouring water on them until skins easily slip off—and cut in fine shreds, one-half teaspoonful extract bitter almonds, one pint flour, one and one-half teaspoonful baking powder, one glass brandy, one-half cupful milk. Rub butter and sugar to a smooth white cream; add eggs, one at a time, beating three or four minutes between each. Sift flour and powder together, add to the butter, etc., with almonds, extract of bitter almonds, brandy and milk; mix into a smooth, medium batter; bake carefully in a rather hot oven twenty minutes.

ROCHESTER JELLY CAKE.

One and one-half cups sugar, two eggs, one-half cup butter, three-fourths cup milk, two heaping cups flour with one teaspoonful cream of tartar, one-half teaspoonful of soda, dissolved in the milk. Put half the above mixture in a small shallow tin, and to the remainder add one teaspoonful molasses, one-half cup raisins (chopped) or currants, one-half teaspoonful cinnamon, cloves, allspice, a little nutmeg and one tablespoonful flour. Bake this in same kind of tins. Put the sheets of cake together, while warm, with jelly between.

FRUIT LAYER CAKE.

This is a delicious novelty in cake-making. Take one cup of sugar, half a cup of butter, one cup and a half of flour, half a cup of wine, one cup of raisins, two eggs and half a teaspoonful of soda; put these ingredients together with care; just as if it were a very rich cake; bake it in three layers and put frosting between—the frosting to be made of the whites of two eggs with enough powdered sugar to make it thick. The top of the cake may be frosted if you choose.

WHIPPED CREAM CAKE.

One cup of sugar and two tablespoonfuls of soft butter stirred together; add the yolks of two eggs well beaten, then add four tablespoonfuls of milk, some flavoring, then the beaten whites of the eggs. Mix a teaspoonful of cream of tartar and half a teaspoon of soda in a cup of flour, sift it into the cake batter and stir lightly. Bake in a small whipping-pan. When the cake is cool, have ready half of a pint of sweet cream sweetened and whipped to a stiff froth, also flavored. Spread it over the cake while fresh. To whip the cream easily, set it on ice before whipping.

ROLLED JELLY CAKE.

Three eggs, one teacup of fine sugar, one teacup of flour; beat the yolks until light, then add the sugar, then add two tablespoonfuls of water, a pinch of salt; lastly stir in the flour, in which there should be a heaping teaspoonful of baking powder. The flour added gradually. Bake in long, shallow biscuit-tins, well greased. Turn out on a damp towel on a bread-board, cover the top with jelly, and roll up while warm.

TO CUT LAYER CAKE.

When cutting Layer Cakes, it is better to first make a round hole in the cake with a knife or tin tube about an inch and a quarter in diameter. This prevents the edge of the cake from crumbling when cutting it.

When making custard filling for Layer Cake always set the dish containing the custard in another dish of boiling water over the fire; this prevents its burning, which would destroy its flavor.

LAYER JELLY CAKE.

Almost any soft cake recipe can be used for jelly cake. The following is excellent: One cup of sugar, half a cup of butter, three eggs, half a cup of sweet milk, two cups of flour, two heaping teaspoonfuls of baking powder, flavoring.

For white, delicate cake the rule for "Silver Cake" is fine; care should be taken, however, that the oven is just right for this cake, as it browns very easily. To be baked in jelly-cake tins in layers, with filling put between when done.

CUSTARD OR CREAM CAKE.

Cream together two cups of sugar and half a cup of butter; add half a cup of sweet milk in which is dissolved half a teaspoonful of soda. Beat the whites of six eggs to a stiff froth and add to the mixture. Have one heaping teaspoonful of cream of tartar stirred thoroughly into three cups of sifted flour and add quickly. Bake in a moderate oven in layers like jelly cake, and, when done, spread custard between.

For the Custard.—Take two cups of sweet milk, put it into a clean suitable dish, set it in a dish of *boiling* water on the range or stove. When the milk comes to a boil add two tablespoonfuls of cornstarch or flour stirred into half a cup of sugar, adding the yolks of four eggs and a little cold milk. Stir this into the boiling milk and when cooked thick enough set aside to cool; afterwards add the flavoring, either vanilla or lemon. It is best to make the custard first, before making the cake part.

HICKORY NUT OR WALNUT CAKE.

Two cups of fine white sugar creamed with half a cup of butter, three eggs, two-thirds of a cup of sweet milk, three cups of sifted flour, one heaping teaspoonful of baking powder sifted through the flour; a tablespoonful (level) of powdered mace, a coffeecup of hickory nut or walnut meats chopped a little. Fill the cake-pans with a layer of the cake, then a layer of raisins upon that, then strew over these a handful of nuts, and so on until the pan is two-thirds full. Line the tins with well-buttered paper and bake in a steady, but not quick, oven. This is most excellent.

CHEAP CREAM CAKE.

One cup of sugar, one egg, one cup sweet milk, two cups flour, one tablespoonful butter, two heaping teaspoonfuls of baking powder; flavor to taste. Divide into three parts and bake in round shallow pans.

Cream.—Beat one egg and one-half cup sugar together, then add one-quarter cup flour, wet with a very little milk and stir this mixture into one-half pint of boiling milk, until thick; flavor to taste. Spread the cream when cool between the cakes.

SOFT GINGER CAKE.

Stir to a cream one cupful of butter and half a cupful of brown sugar; add to this two cupfuls of cooking molasses, a cupful of sweet milk, a tablespoonful of ginger, a teaspoonful of ground cinnamon; beat all thoroughly together, then add three eggs, the whites and yolks beaten separately; beat into this two cups of sifted flour, then a teaspoonful of soda dissolved in a spoonful of water and last, two more cupfuls of sifted flour. Butter and paper two common square bread-pans, divide the mixture and pour half into each. Bake in a moderate oven. This cake requires long and slow baking, from forty to sixty minutes. I find that if sour milk is used the cakes are much lighter, but either sweet or sour is most excellent.

HARD GINGERBREAD.

Made the same as "Soft Gingerbread," omitting the eggs and mixing hard enough to roll out like biscuit; rolled nearly half an inch thick and cut out like small biscuits, or it can be baked in a sheet or on a biscuit-tin; cut slits a quarter of an inch deep across the top of the tin from side to side. When baked and while hot, rub over the top with molasses and let it dry on.

These two recipes are the best I have ever found among a large variety that I have tried, the ingredients giving the best proportion for flavor and excellence.

PLAIN GINGERBREAD.

One cup of *dark* cooking molasses, one cup of sour cream, one teaspoonful of soda dissolved in a little warm water, a teaspoonful of salt and one heaping teaspoonful of ginger; make about as thick as cup cake. To be eaten warm.

WHITE GINGER BISCUIT.

One cup of butter, two cups of sugar, one cup of sour cream or milk, three eggs, one teaspoonful of soda dissolved in a tablespoonful of warm water, one tablespoonful of ginger, one teaspoonful of ground cinnamon and five cups of sifted flour, or enough to roll out *soft*. Cut out rather thick like biscuits; brush over the tops, while hot, with the white of an egg, or sprinkle with sugar while hot.

The grated rind and the juice of an orange add much to the flavor of ginger cake.

GOLD AND SILVER CAKE.

This cake is baked in layers like jelly cake. Divide the silver cake batter and color it pink with a little cochineal; this gives you pink, white and yellow layers. Put together with frosting. Frost the top.

This can be put together like marble cake, first a spoonful of one kind, then another, until the dish is full.

BOSTON CREAM CAKES.

Put into a large-sized saucepan half a cup of butter and one cup of hot water; set it on the fire; when the mixture begins to boil, turn in a pint of sifted flour at once, beat and work it well with a vegetable masher until it is very smooth. Remove from the fire, and when cool enough add five eggs that have been well beaten, first the yolks and then the whites, also half a teaspoonful of soda and a teaspoonful of salt. Drop on buttered tins in large spoonfuls about two inches apart. Bake in a quick oven about fifteen minutes. When done and quite cold, open them on the side with a knife or scissors and put in as much of the custard as possible.

Cream for Filling.—Made of two eggs, three tablespoonfuls of sifted flour (or half cup of cornstarch) and one cup of sugar. Put two-thirds of a pint of milk over the fire in a double boiler; in a third of a pint of milk, stir the sugar, flour and beaten eggs. As soon as the milk looks like boiling, pour in the mixture and stir briskly for three minutes, until it thickens; then remove from the fire and add a teaspoonful of butter; when cool, flavor with vanilla or lemon and fill your cakes.

CHOCOLATE ECLAIRS.

Make the mixture exactly like the recipe for "Boston Cream Cakes." Spread it on buttered pans in oblong pieces about four inches long and one and a half wide, to be laid about two inches apart; they must be baked in a rather quick oven about twenty-five minutes. As soon as baked ice with chocolate icing, and when this is cold split them on one side and fill with the same cream as "Boston Cream Cakes."

HUCKLEBERRY CAKE.

Beat a cup of butter and two cups of sugar together until light, then add a half cup of milk, four eggs beaten separately, the yolks to a cream and the whites to a stiff froth, one teaspoonful of grated nutmeg, the same of cinnamon and two teaspoonfuls of baking powder. The baking powder to be rubbed into the flour. Bub one quart of huckleberries well with some flour and add them last, but do not mash them. Pour into buttered pans, about an inch thick; dust the tops with sugar and bake. It is better the day after baking.

SWEET STRAWBERRY CAKE.

Three eggs, one cupful of sugar, two of flour, one tablespoonful of butter, a teaspoonful, heaped, of baking powder. Beat the butter and sugar together and add the eggs well beaten. Stir in the flour and baking powder well sifted together. Bake in deep tin plate. This quantity will fill four plates. With three pints of strawberries mix a cupful of sugar and mash them a little. Spread the fruit between the layers of cake. The top layer of strawberries may be covered with a meringue made with the white of an egg and a tablespoonful of powdered sugar.

Save out the largest berries and arrange them around in circles on the top in the white frosting. Makes a very fancy dish, as well as a most delicious cake.

MOLASSES CUP CAKES.

One cup of butter, one of sugar, six eggs, five cupfuls of sifted flour, one tablespoonful of cinnamon, two tablespoonfuls of ginger, three teacupfuls of cooking molasses and one heaping teaspoonful of soda. Stir the butter and sugar to a cream; beat the eggs very light, the yolks and whites separately, and add to it; after which put in the spices; then the molasses and flour in rotation, stirring the mixture all the time; beat the whole *well* before adding the soda and but little afterwards. Put into well-buttered patty-pan tins and bake in a *very moderate* oven. A baker's recipe.

BAKERS' GINGER SNAPS.

Boil all together the following ingredients: Two cups of brown sugar, two cups of cooking molasses, one cup of shortening, which should be part butter, one *large* tablespoonful of ginger, one tablespoonful of ground cinnamon, one teaspoonful of cloves; remove from the fire and let it cool. In the meantime, sift four cups of flour and stir part of it into the above mixture. Now dissolve a teaspoonful of soda in a tablespoonful of warm water and beat into this mixture, stir in the remainder of the flour and make stiff enough to roll into long rolls about an inch in diameter, and cut off from the end into half-inch pieces. Place them on well-buttered tins, giving plenty of room to spread. Bake in a moderate oven. Let them cool before taking out of the tins.

GINGER COOKIES.

One cup sugar, one cup molasses, one cup butter, one egg, one tablespoonful vinegar, one tablespoonful ginger, one teaspoonful soda dissolved in boiling water, mix like cooky dough, rather soft.

GINGER SNAPS.

One cup brown sugar, two cups molasses, one large cup butter, two teaspoonfuls soda, two teaspoonfuls ginger, three pints flour to commence with; rub shortening and sugar together into the flour; add enough more flour to roll very smooth, very thin, and bake in a quick oven. The dough can be kept for days by putting it in the flour barrel under the flour, and bake a few at a time The more flour that can be worked in and the smoother they can be rolled, the better and more brittle they will be. Should be rolled out to wafer-like thinness. Bake quickly without burning. They should become perfectly cold before putting aside.

DOMINOES.

Have a plain cake baked in rather thin sheets and cut into small oblong pieces the size and shape of a domino, a trifle larger. Frost the top and sides. When the frosting is hard, draw the black lines and make the dots with a small brush dipped in melted chocolate. These are very nice for children's parties.

FANCY CAKES.

These delicious little fancy cakes may be made by making a rich jumble-paste—rolling out in any desired shape; cut some paste in thick, narrow strips and lay around your cakes, so as to form a deep, cup-like edge; place on a well-buttered tin and bake. When done, fill with iced fruit prepared as follows: Take rich, ripe peaches (canned ones will do if fine and well drained from all juice) cut in halves; plums, strawberries, pineapples cut in squares or small triangles, or any other available fruit, and dip in the white of an egg that has been very slightly beaten and then in pulverized sugar, and lay in the centre of your cakes.

WAFERS.

Dissolve four ounces of butter in half a teacup of milk; stir together four ounces of white sugar, eight ounces of sifted flour and the yolk of one egg, adding gradually the butter and milk, a tablespoonful of orange-flour water and a pinch of salt; mix it well. Heat the wafer-irons, butter their inner surfaces, put in a tablespoonful of the batter and close the irons immediately; put the irons over the fire, and turn them occasionally, until the wafer is cooked; when the wafers are all cooked roll them on a small round stick, stand them upon a sieve and dry them; serve with ices.

PEACH CAKES.

Take the yolks and whites of five eggs and beat them separately (the whites to a stiff froth.) Then mix the beaten yolks with half a pound of pulverized and sifted loaf or crushed sugar, and beat the two together thoroughly. Fifteen minutes will be none too long for the latter operation if you would have excellence with your cakes.

Now add half a pound of fine flour, dredging it in a little at a time, and then put in the whites of the eggs, beating the whole together for four or five minutes. Then with a large spoon, drop the batter upon a baking tin, which has been buttered and floured, being careful to have the cakes as nearly the same size as possible and resembling in shape the half of a peach. Have a quick oven ready and bake the cakes about ten minutes, watching them closely so that they may only come to a light brown color. Then take them out, spread the flat side of each with peach jam, and stick them together in pairs, covering the outside with a thin coat of icing, which when dry can be brushed over on one side of the cake, with a little cochineal water.

CUP CAKES.

Two cups of sugar, one cup of butter, one cup of milk, three cups and a half of flour and four eggs, half a teaspoonful of soda, large spoon cream of tartar; stir butter and sugar together and add the beaten yolks of the eggs, then the milk, then flavoring and the whites. Put cream of tartar in flour and add last. Bake in buttered gem-pans, or drop the batter, a teaspoonful at a time, in rows on flat buttered tins.

To this recipe may be added a cup of English currants or chopped raisins; and also another variety of cake may be made by adding a half cup citron sliced and floured, a half cupful of chopped almonds and lemon extract.

VARIEGATED CAKES.

One cup powdered sugar, one-half cup of butter creamed with the sugar, one-half cup of milk, four eggs, the whites only, whipped light, two and one-half cups prepared flour. Bitter almond flavoring, spinach juice and cochineal. Cream the butter and sugar; add the milk, flavoring, the whites and flour. Divide the batter into three parts. Bruise and pound a few leaves of spinach in a thin muslin bag until you can express the juice. Put a few drops of this into one portion of the batter, color another with cochineal, leaving the third white. Put a little of each into small, round pans or cups, giving a light stir to each color as you add the next. This will vein the cakes prettily. Put the white between the pink and green, that the tints may show better. If you can get pistachio nuts to pound up for the green, the cakes will be much nicer. Ice on sides and top.

CORNSTARCH CAKES.

One cupful each of butter and sweet milk and half a cup of cornstarch, two cupfuls each of sugar and flour, the whites of five eggs beaten to a stiff froth, two teaspoonfuls of cream of tartar and one of soda; flavor to taste. Bake in gem-tins or patty-pans.

SPONGE DROPS.

Beat to a froth three eggs and one teacup of sugar; stir into this one heaping coffeecup of flour, in which one teaspoonful of cream of tartar and half a teaspoonful of saleratus are thoroughly mixed. Flavor with lemon. Butter tin sheets with washed butter and drop in teaspoonfuls about three inches apart. Bake instantly in a very quick oven. Watch closely as they will burn easily. Serve with ice cream.

SAVORY BISCUITS OR LADY FINGERS.

Put nine tablespoonfuls of fine white sugar into a bowl and put the bowl into hot water to heat the sugar; when the sugar is thoroughly heated, break nine eggs into the bowl and beat them quickly until they become a little warm and rather thick; then take the bowl from the water and continue beating until it is nearly or quite cold; now stir in lightly nine tablespoonfuls of sifted flour; then with a paper funnel, or something of the kind, lay this mixture out upon papers, in biscuits three inches long and half an inch thick, in the form of fingers; sift sugar over the biscuits and bake them upon tins to a light brown; when they are done and cold, remove them from the papers, by wetting them on the back; dry them and they are ready for use. They are often used in making Charlotte Russe.

PASTRY SANDWICHES.

Puff paste, jam of any kind, the white of an egg, sifted sugar.

Roll the paste out thin; put half of it on a baking sheet or tin, and spread equally over it apricot, greengage, or any preserve that may be preferred. Lay over this preserve another thin paste, press the edges together all round, and mark the paste in lines with a knife on the surface, to show where to cut it when baked. Bake from twenty minutes to half an hour; and, a short time before being done, take the pastry out of the oven, brush it over with the white of an egg, sift over pounded sugar and put it back in the oven to color. When cold, cut it into strips; pile these on a dish pyramidically and serve.

This may be made of jelly-cake dough, and, after baking, allowed to cool before spreading with the preserve; either way is good, as well as fanciful.

NEAPOLITAINES.

One cup of powdered sugar, half a cup of butter, two tablespoonfuls of lemon juice, three whole eggs and three yolks, beaten separately, three cups of sifted flour. Put this all together with half a teaspoonful of soda dissolved in a tablespoonful of milk. If it is too stiff to roll out, add just enough more milk. Roll it a quarter of an inch thick and cut it out with any tin cutter. Place the cakes in a pan slightly greased and color the tops with beaten egg and milk, with some chopped almonds over them. Bake in a rather quick oven.

BRUNSWICK JELLY CAKES.

Stir one cup of powdered white sugar and one-half cup of butter together, till perfectly light; beat the yolks of three eggs till very thick and smooth; sift three cups of flour and stir it into the beaten eggs with the butter and sugar; add a teaspoonful of mixed spice (nutmeg, mace and cinnamon) and half a glass of rose-water or wine; stir the whole well and lay it on your paste-board, which must first be sprinkled with flour; if you find it so moist as to be unmanageable, throw in a little more flour; spread the dough into a sheet about half an inch thick and cut it out in round cakes with a biscuit-cutter; lay them in buttered pans and bake about five or six minutes; when cold, spread over the surface of each cake a liquor of fruit jelly or marmalade; then beat the whites of three or four eggs till they stand alone; beat into the froth, by degrees, a sufficiency of powdered loaf sugar to make it as thick as icing; flavor with a few drops of strong essence of lemon, and with a spoon heap it up on each cake, making it high in the centre; put the cakes into a cool oven, and as soon as the tops are colored a pale brown, take them out.

LITTLE PLUM CAKES.

One cup of sugar and half a cup of butter beaten to a smooth cream; add three well-beaten eggs, a teaspoonful of vanilla extract, four cups of sifted flour, one cup of raisins and one of currants, half of a teaspoonful of baking soda dissolved in a little water, and milk enough to make a stiff batter; drop this batter in drops on well-buttered tins and bake in a *quick* oven.

JUMBLES.

Cream together two cups of sugar and one of butter, add three well-beaten eggs and six tablespoonfuls of sweet milk, two teaspoonfuls of baking powder, flavor to taste, flour enough to make into a soft dough; do not roll it on the paste-board, but break off pieces of dough the size of a walnut and make into rings by rolling out rolls as large as your finger, and joining the ends; lay them on tins to bake, an inch apart, as it rises and spreads; bake in a *moderate* oven. These jumbles are very delicate and will keep a long time.

WINE JUMBLES.

One cup of butter, two of sugar, three eggs, one wine-glass of wine, one spoonful of vanilla and flour enough to roll out. Roll as thin as the blade of a knife and cut with an oval cutter. Bake on tin-sheets in a quick oven until a dark brown. These will keep a year if kept in a tin box and in a dry place.

COCOANUT JUMBLES.

Grate one large cupful of cocoanut; rub one cupful of butter with one and a half cupfuls of sugar; add three beaten eggs, whites and yolks separately, two tablespoonfuls of milk and five cupfuls of sifted flour; then add by degrees the grated nut, so as to make a stiff dough, rolled thin and cut with a round cutter, having a hole in the middle. Bake in a quick oven from five to ten minutes.

PHILADELPHIA JUMBLES.

Two cups of sugar, one cup of butter, eight eggs beaten light; essence of bitter almond or rose to taste; enough flour to enable you to roll them out.

Stir the sugar and butter to a light cream, then add the well-whipped eggs, the flavoring and flour; mix well together, roll out in powdered sugar in a sheet a quarter of an inch thick; cut into rings with a jagging-iron and bake in a quick oven on buttered tins.

ALMOND JUMBLES.

Three cupfuls of soft sugar, two cupfuls of flour, half a cupful of butter, one teacupful of loppered milk, five eggs well beaten, two tablespoonfuls of rose-water, three-quarters of a pound of almonds, blanched and chopped *very* fine, one teaspoonful of soda dissolved in boiling water.

Cream butter and sugar; stir in the beaten yolks the milk, flour, rose-water, almonds and, lastly, the beaten whites very lightly and quickly; drop in rings on buttered paper and bake at once.

FRUIT JUMBLES.

Two cups of sugar, one cup of butter, five cupfuls of flour, five eggs, one small teacupful of milk, in which dissolve half a teaspoonful of soda; cream the butter, add the sugar, cream again; then add yolks of eggs, the milk, beaten whites and flour; a little cinnamon, nutmeg, allspice and ground cloves and one-quarter of a pound of currants, rolled in flour.

COOKIES.

One cup of butter, two cups of sugar, a *small* teacupful of sweet milk, half a grated nutmeg and five cups of sifted flour, in which there has been sifted with it two teaspoonfuls of baking powder; mix into a soft dough and cut into round cakes; roll the dough as thin as pie crust. Bake in a quick oven a light brown. These can be made of sour milk and a teaspoonful of soda dissolved in it, or sour or sweet cream can be used in place of butter.

Water cookies made the same as above, using water in place of milk. Water cookies keep longer than milk cookies.

FAVORITE COOKIES.

One cup of butter, one and a half cups of sugar, one-half cup of sour milk one level teaspoonful of soda, a teaspoonful of grated nutmeg Flour enough to roll; make quite soft. Put a tablespoonful of fine sugar on a plate and dip the tops of each as you cut them out. Place on buttered tins and bake in a quick oven a light brown.

FRUIT COOKIES.

One cupful and a half of sugar, one cupful of butter, one-half cup of sweet milk, one egg, two teaspoonfuls of baking powder, a teaspoonful of grated nutmeg, three tablespoonfuls of English currants or chopped raisins. Mix soft and roll out, using just enough flour to stiffen sufficiently. Cut out with a large cutter, wet the tops with milk and sprinkle sugar over them. Bake on buttered tins in a quick oven.

CRISP COOKIES. (Very Nice.)

One cup of butter, two cups of sugar, three eggs well beaten, a teaspoonful of soda and two of cream of tartar, spoonful of milk, one teaspoonful of nutmeg and one of cinnamon. Flour enough to make a soft dough just stiff enough to roll out. Try a pint of sifted flour to begin with, working it in gradually. Spread a little sweet milk over each and sprinkle with sugar. Bake in a quick oven a light brown.

LEMON COOKIES.

Four cups of sifted flour, or enough for a stiff dough, one teacupful of butter, two cups of sugar, the juice of one lemon and the grated peel from the outside, three eggs whipped very light. Beat thoroughly each ingredient, adding, after all is in, a half teaspoonful of soda dissolved in a tablespoonful of milk. Roll out as any cookies and bake a light brown. Use no other wetting.

COCOANUT COOKIES.

One cup grated cocoanut, one and one-half cups sugar, three-fourths cup butter, one-half cup milk, two eggs, one large teaspoonful baking powder, one-half teaspoonful extract of vanilla and flour enough to roll out.

DOUGHNUTS OR FRIED CAKES.

Success in making good fried cakes depends as much on the *cooking* as the mixing. In the first place, there should be boiling lard enough to free them from the bottom of the kettle, so that they swim on the top, and the lard should never be so hot as to smoke or so cool as not to be at the boiling point; if it is, they soak grease and are spoiled. If it is at the right heat, the doughnuts will in about ten minutes be of a delicate brown outside and nicely cooked inside. Five or six minutes will cook a cruller. Try the fat by dropping a bit of the dough in first; if it is right, the fat will boil up when it is dropped in. They should be turned over almost constantly, which causes them to rise and brown evenly. When they are sufficiently cooked, raise them from the hot fat and drain them until every drop ceases dripping.

CRULLERS OR FRIED CAKES.

One and a half cupfuls of sugar, one cupful of sour milk, two eggs, two scant tablespoonfuls of melted butter, half a nutmeg grated, a large teaspoonful of cinnamon, a teaspoonful of salt and one of soda; make a little stiffer than biscuit dough, roll out a quarter of an inch thick, and cut with a fried-cake cutter, with a hole in the centre. Fry in hot lard.

These can be made with sweet milk and baking powder, using two heaping teaspoonfuls of the baking powder in place of soda.

RAISED DOUGHNUTS.

Old-fashioned "raised doughnuts" are seldom seen nowadays, but are easily made. Make a sponge as for bread, using a pint of warm water or milk, and a large half cupful of yeast; when the sponge is very light, add half a cupful of butter or sweet lard, a coffeecupful of sugar, a teaspoonful of salt and one small teaspoonful of soda dissolved in a little water, one tablespoonful of cinnamon, a little grated nutmeg; stir in now two well-beaten eggs, add sifted flour until it is the consistency of biscuit dough, knead it well, cover and let rise; then roll the dough out into a sheet half an inch thick, cut out with a very small biscuit-cutter, or in strips half an inch wide and three inches long, place them on greased tins, cover them well and let them rise before frying them. Drop them in very hot lard. Raised cakes require longer time than cakes made with baking powder. Sift powdered sugar over them as fast as they are fried, while warm. Our grandmothers put allspice into these cakes; that, however, is a matter of taste.

BAKERS' RAISED DOUGHNUTS.

Warm a teacupful of lard in a pint of milk; when nearly cool add enough flour to make a thick batter and add a small cupful of yeast; beat it well and set it to rise; when light work in gradually and carefully three cupfuls of sugar, the whipped whites of six eggs, half a teaspoonful of soda dissolved in a spoonful of milk, one teaspoonful of salt, a teaspoonful of ground cinnamon and half of a nutmeg grated; then work in gradually enough flour to make it stiff enough to roll out; let it rise again and when very light roll it out in a sheet an inch thick; cut into rounds; put into the centre of each round a large Sultana raisin, seeded, and mold into perfectly round balls; flatten a little; let them stand a few minutes before boiling them; have plenty of lard in the pot and when it boils drop in the cakes; when they are a light, brown take them out with a perforated skimmer; drain on soft white paper and roll, while warm, in fine powdered sugar.

Purcell's Bakery, New York City.

CRULLERS OR WONDERS.

Three eggs, three tablespoonfuls of melted lard or butter, three tablespoonfuls of sugar; mix very hard with sifted flour, as hard as can be rolled, and to be rolled very thin like pie crust; cut in squares three inches long and two wide, then cut several slits or lines lengthwise to within a quarter of an inch of the edges of the ends; run your two forefingers through every other slit; lay them down on the board edgewise and dent them. These are very dainty when fried. Fry in hot lard a light brown.

GERMAN DOUGHNUTS.

One pint of milk; four eggs, one small tablespoonful of melted butter, flavoring, salt to taste; first boil the milk and pour it, while hot, over a pint of flour; beat it very smooth and when it is cool have ready the yolks of the eggs well beaten; add them to the milk and flour, beaten well into it, then add the well-beaten whites; then, lastly, add the salt and as much more flour as will make the whole into a soft dough; flour your board, turn your dough upon it, roll it in pieces as thick as your finger and turn them in the form of a ring; cook in plenty of boiling lard. A nice breakfast cake with coffee.

CUTTING PUMPKIN FOR PIES.

CUTTING PUMPKIN FOR PIES.

NUT CAKES. (Fried.)

Beat two eggs well, add to them one ounce of sifted sugar, two ounces of warmed butter, two tablespoonfuls of yeast, a teacupful of luke-warm milk and a little salt. Whip all well together, then stir in by degrees one pound of flour, and, if requisite, more milk, making thin dough. Beat it until it falls from the spoon, then set it to rise. When it has risen make butter or lard hot in a frying pan, cut from the light dough little pieces the size of a walnut, and, without molding or kneading, fry them pale brown. As they are done lay them on a napkin to absorb any of the fat.

TRIFLES.

Work one egg and a tablespoonful of sugar to as much flour as will make a stiff paste; roll it as thin as a dollar piece and cut it into small round or square cakes; drop two or three at a time into the boiling lard; when they rise to the surface and turn over they are done; take them out with a skimmer and lay them on an inverted sieve to drain. When served for dessert or supper put a spoonful of jelly on each.

PUFF-BALL DOUGHNUTS.

These doughnuts, eaten fresh and warm, are a delicious breakfast dish and are quickly made. Three eggs, one cupful of sugar, a pint of sweet milk, salt, nutmeg and flour enough to permit the spoon to stand upright in the mixture; add two heaping teaspoonfuls of baking powder to the flour; beat all until very light. Drop by the dessertspoonful into boiling lard. These will not absorb a bit of fat and are not at all rich and consequently are the least injurious of this kind of cakes.

PASTRY, PIES AND TARTS.

GENERAL REMARKS.

Use the very best materials in making pastry; the shortening should be fresh, sweet and hard; the water cold (ice-water is best), the paste rolled on a cold board and all handled as little as possible. When the crust is made, it makes it much more flaky and puff much more to put it in a dish covered with a cloth and set in a very cold place for half an hour, or even an hour; in summer, it could be placed in the ice box.

A great improvement is made in pie crust by the addition of about a heaping teaspoonful of baking powder to a quart of flour, also brushing the paste as often as rolled out, and the pieces of butter placed thereon, with the white of an egg, assists it to rise in *leaves* or *flakes*. As this is the great beauty of puff paste, it is as well to try this method.

If currants are to be used in pies, they should be carefully picked over and washed in several waters, dried in a towel and dredged with flour before they are suitable for use.

Raisins, and all dried fruits for pies and cakes, should be seeded stoned and dredged with flour before using.

Almonds should be blanched by pouring boiling water upon them and then slipping the skin off with the fingers. In pounding them, always add a little rose or orange-water, with fine sugar, to prevent their becoming oily.

Great care is requisite in heating an oven for baking pastry. If you can hold your hand in the heated oven while you count twenty, the oven has just the proper temperature and it should be kept at this temperature as long as the pastry is in; this heat will bake to a light brown and will give the pastry a fresh and flaky appearance. If you suffer the heat to abate, the under crust will become heavy and clammy and the upper crust will fall in.

Another good way to ascertain when the oven is heated to the proper degree for puff paste: put a small piece of the paste in previous to baking the whole, and then the heat can thus be judged of.

Pie crust can be kept a week, and the last be better than the if put in a tightly covered dish and set in the ice chest in summer and in a cool place in winter, and thus you can make a fresh pie every day with little trouble.

In baking custard, pumpkin or squash pies, it is well, in order that the mixture may not be absorbed by the paste, to first partly bake the paste before adding it, and when stewed fruit is used the filling should be perfectly cool when put in, or it will make the bottom crust sodden.

HOW TO MAKE A PIE.

After making the crust, take a portion of it, roll it out and fit it to a buttered pie-plate by cutting it off evenly around the edge; gather up the scraps left from cutting and make into another sheet for the top crust; roll it a little thinner than the under crust; lap one-half over the other and cut three or four slits about a quarter of an inch from the folded edge (this prevents the steam from escaping through the rim of the pie, and causing the juices to run out from the edges). Now fill your pie-plate with your prepared filling, wet the top edge of the rim, lay the upper crust across the centre of the pie, turn back the half that is lapped over, seal the two edges together by slightly pressing down with your thumb, then notch evenly and regularly with a three-tined fork, dipping occasionally in flour to prevent sticking. Bake in a rather quick oven a light brown, and until the filling boils up through the slits in the upper crust.

To prevent the juice soaking through into the crust, making it soggy wet the under crust with the white of an egg, just before you put in the pie mixture. If the top of the pie is brushed over with the egg, it gives it a beautiful glaze.

FOR ICING PASTRY.

To ice pastry, which is the usual method adopted for fruit tarts and sweet dishes of pastry, put the white of an egg on a plate and with the blade of a knife beat it to a stiff froth. When the pastry is nearly baked, brush it over with this and sift over some pounded sugar; put it back into the oven to set the glaze and in a few minutes it will be done. Great care should be taken that the paste does not catch or burn in the oven, which is very liable to do after the icing is laid on.

Or make a meringue by adding a tablespoonful of white sugar to the beaten white of one egg. Spread over the top and slightly brown in the oven.

FINE PUFF PASTE.

Into one quart of sifted flour mix two teaspoonfuls of baking powder and a teaspoonful of salt; *then sift again*. Measure out one teacupful of butter and one of lard, hard and cold. Take the lard and rub into the flour until a very fine smooth paste. Then put in just enough *ice-water*, say half a cupful, containing a beaten white of egg, to mix a very stiff dough. Boll it out into a thin sheet, spread with one-fourth of the butter, sprinkle over with a little flour, then roll up closely in a long roll, like a scroll, double the ends towards the centre, flatten and re-roll, then spread again with another quarter of the butter. Repeat this operation until the butter is used up. Put it on an earthen dish, cover it with a cloth and set it in a cold place, in the ice box in summer; let it remain until *cold*; an hour or more before making out the crust. Tarts made with this paste cannot be cut with a knife when fresh; they go into flakes at the touch.

You may roll this pastry in any direction, from you, toward you, sideways, any way, it matters not, but you must have nice flour, *ice-water* and very *little* of it, and strength to roll it, if you would succeed.

This recipe I purchased from a colored cook on one of the Lake Michigan steamers many years ago, and it is, without exception, the finest puff paste I have ever seen.

PUFF PASTE FOR PIES.

One quart of pastry flour, one pint of butter, one tablespoonful of salt, one of sugar, one and a quarter cupfuls of ice-water. Wash the hands with soap and water and dip them first in very hot and then in cold water. Rinse a large bowl or pan with boiling water and then with cold. Half fill it with cold water. Wash the butter in this, working it with the hands until it is light and waxy. This frees it from the salt and buttermilk and lightens it, so that the pastry is more delicate. Shape the butter into two thin cakes and put in a pan of ice-water to harden. Mix the salt and sugar with the flour. With the hands, rub one-third of the butter into the flour. Add the water, stirring with a knife. Stir quickly and vigorously until the paste is a smooth ball. Sprinkle the board *lightly* with flour. Turn the paste on this and pound quickly and lightly with the rolling-pin. Do not break the paste. Roll from you and to one side; or if easier to roll from you all the time, turn the paste around. When it is about one-fourth of an inch thick, wipe the remaining butter, break it in bits and spread these on the paste. Sprinkle lightly with flour. Fold the paste, one-third from each side, so that the edges meet. Now fold from the ends, but do not have these meet. Double the paste, pound lightly and roll down to about one-third of an inch in thickness. Fold as before and roll down again. Repeat this three times if for pies and six times if for *vol-au-vents*, patties, tarts, etc. Place on the ice to harden, when it has been rolled the last time. It should be in the ice chest at least an hour before being used. In hot weather, if the paste sticks when being rolled down, put it on a tin sheet and place on ice. As soon as it is chilled, it will roll easily. The less flour you use in rolling out the paste, the tenderer it will be. No matter how carefully every part of the work may be done, the paste will not be good if much flour is used.

Maria Parloa.

SOYER'S RECIPE FOR PUFF PASTE.

To every pound of flour allow the yolk of one egg, the juice of one lemon, half a saltspoonful of salt, cold water, one pound of fresh butter.

Put the flour onto the paste-board; make a hole in the centre, into which put the yolk of the egg, the lemon juice and salt; mix the whole with cold water (this should be iced in summer if convenient) into a soft, flexible paste with the right hand, and handle it as little as possible; then squeeze all the buttermilk from the butter, wring it in a cloth and roll out the paste; place the butter on this and fold the edges of the paste over, so as to hide it; roll it out again to the thickness of a quarter of an inch; fold over one-third, over which again pass the rolling-pin; then fold over the other third, thus forming a square; place it with the ends, top and bottom before you, shaking a little flour both under and over, and repeat the rolls and turns twice again as before. Flour a baking-sheet, put the paste on this and let it remain on ice or in some cool place for half an hour; then roll twice more, turning it as before; place it again upon the ice for a quarter of an hour, give it two more rolls, making seven in all, and it is ready for use when required.

RULE FOR UNDER CRUST.

A good rule for pie crust for a pie requiring only an under crust, as a custard or pumpkin pie, is: Three *large* tablespoonfuls of flour sifted, rubbing into it a *large* tablespoonful of cold butter, or part butter and part lard, and a pinch of salt, mixing with *cold* water enough to form a smooth, stiff paste, and rolled quite thin.

PLAIN PIE CRUST.

Two and a half cupfuls of sifted flour, one cupful of shortening, half butter and half lard cold, a pinch of salt, a heaping teaspoonful of baking powder sifted through the flour. Rub thoroughly the shortening into the flour. Mix together with half a teacupful of *cold* water, or enough to form a rather stiff dough; mix as little as possible, just enough to get it into shape to roll out; it must be handled very lightly. This rule is for two pies.

When you have a little pie crust left do not throw it away; roll it thin, cut in small squares and bake. Just before tea put a spoonful of raspberry jelly on each square.

PUFF PASTE OF SUET.

Two cupfuls of flour, one-half teaspoonful of salt, one teaspoonful of baking powder, one cup of chopped suet, freed of skin, and chopped very fine, one cupful of water. Place the flour, sifted with the powder in a bowl, add suet and water; mix into smooth, rather firm dough.

This paste is excellent for fruit puddings and dumplings that are boiled; if it is well made, it will be light and flaky and the suet imperceptible. It is also excellent for meat pies, baked or boiled. All the ingredients should be very cold when mixing, and the suet dredged with flour after it is chopped, to prevent the particles from adhering to each other.

POTATO CRUST.

Boil and mash a dozen medium-sized potatoes, add one good teaspoonful of salt, two tablespoonfuls of cold butter and half a cupful of milk or cream. Stiffen with flour sufficient to roll out. Nice for the tops of meat pies.

TO MAKE PIE CRUST FLAKY.

In making a pie, after you have rolled out your top crust, cut it about the right size, spread it over with butter, then shake sifted flour over the butter, enough to cover it well. Cut a slit in the middle place it over the top of your pie, and fasten the edges as any pie. Now take the pie on your left hand and a dipper of cold water in your right hand; tip the pie slanting a little, pour over the water sufficiently to rinse off the flour. Enough flour will stick to the butter to fry into the crust, to give it a fine, blistered, flaky look, which many cooks think is much better than rolling the butter into the crust.

TARTLETS. No. 1.

Tarts of strawberry or any other kind of preserves are generally made of the trimmings of puff paste rolled a little thicker than the ordinary pies; then cut out with a round cutter, first dipped in hot water, to make the edges smooth, and placed in small tart-pans, first pricking a few holes at the bottom with a fork before placing them in the oven. Bake from ten to fifteen minutes. Let the paste cool a little; then fill it with preserve. By this manner, both the flavor and color of the jam are preserved, which would be lost were it baked in the oven on the paste; and, besides, so much jam is not required.

TARTLETS. No. 2.

Tartlets are nice made in this manner: Roll some good puff paste out thin, and cut it into two and a half inch squares; brush each square over with the white of an egg, then fold down the corners, so that they all meet in the middle of each piece of paste; slightly press the two pieces together, brush them over with the egg, sift over sugar and bake in a nice quick oven for about a quarter of an hour. When they are done, make a little hole in the middle of the paste and fill it up with apricot jam, marmalade, or red currant jelly. Pile them high in the centre of a dish on a napkin and garnish with the same preserves the tartlets are filled with.

PATTIES, OR SHELLS FOR TARTS.

Roll out a nice puff paste thin; cut out with a glass or cookie-cutter and with a wine-glass or smaller cutter, cut out the centre of two out of three; lay the rings thus made on the third, and bake at once. May be used for veal or oyster patties, or filled with jelly, jam or preserves, as tarts. Or shells may be made by lining patty-pans with paste. If the paste is light, the shells will be fine. Filled with jelly and covered with meringue (tablespoonful of sugar to the white of one egg) and browned in oven, they are very nice to serve for tea.

If the cutters are dipped in *hot water*, the edges of the tartlets will rise much higher and smoother when baking.

TARTS.

Larger pans are required for tarts proper, the size of small, shallow pie-tins; then after the paste is baked and cooled and filled with the jam or preserve, a few stars or leaves are placed on the top, or strips of paste, criss-crossed on the top, all of which have been previously baked on a tin by themselves.

Dried fruit, stewed until thick, makes fine tart pies, also cranberries stewed and well sweetened.

GREEN APPLE PIE.

Peel, core and slice tart apples enough for a pie; sprinkle over about three tablespoonfuls of sugar, a teaspoonful of cinnamon, a small level tablespoonful of sifted flour, two tablespoonfuls of water, a few bits of butter, stir all together with a spoon; put it into a pie-tin lined with pie paste; cover with a top crust and bake about forty minutes.

The result will be a delicious, juicy pie.

APPLE CUSTARD PIE. No. 1.

Three cupfuls of milk, four eggs and one cupful of sugar, two cupfuls of thick stewed apples, strained through a colander. Beat the whites and yolks of the eggs lightly and mix the yolks well with the apples, flavoring with nutmeg. Then beat into this the milk and, lastly, the whites. Let the crust partly bake before turning in this filling. To be baked with only the one crust, like all custard pies.

APPLE CUSTARD PIE. No. 2.

Select fair sweet apples, pare and grate them, and to every teacupful of the apple add two eggs well beaten, two tablespoonfuls of fine sugar, one of melted butter, the grated rind and half the juice of one lemon, half a wine-glass of brandy and one teacupful of milk; mix all well and pour into a deep plate lined with paste; put a strip of the paste around the edge of the dish and bake thirty minutes.

APPLE CUSTARD PIE. No. 3.

Lay a crust in your plates; slice apples thin and half fill your plates; pour over them a custard made of four eggs and one quart of milk, sweetened and seasoned to your taste.

APPLE CUSTARD PIE. No. 4.

Peel sour apples and stew until soft, and not much water left in them; then rub through a colander; beat three eggs for each pie to be baked and put in at the rate of one cupful of butter and one of sugar for three pies; season with nutmeg.

IRISH APPLE PIE.

Pare and take out the cores of the apples, cutting each apple into four or eight pieces, according to their size. Lay them neatly in a baking dish, seasoning them with brown sugar and any spice, such as pounded cloves and cinnamon, or grated lemon peel. A little quince marmalade gives a fine flavor to the pie. Add a little water and cover with puff paste. Bake for an hour.

MOCK APPLE PIE.

Crush finely with a rolling pin, one large Boston cracker; put it into a bowl and pour upon it one teacupful of cold water; add one teacupful of fine white sugar, the juice and pulp of one lemon, half a lemon rind grated and a little nutmeg; line the pie-plate with half puff paste, pour in the mixture, cover with the paste and bake half an hour.

These are proportions for one pie.

APPLE AND PEACH MERINGUE PIE.

Stew the apples or peaches and sweeten to taste. Mash smooth and season with nutmeg. Fill the crusts and bake until just done. Put on no top crust. Take the whites of three eggs for each pie and whip to a stiff froth, and sweeten with three tablespoonfuls of powdered sugar. Flavor with rose-water or vanilla; beat until it will stand alone; then spread it on the pie one-half to one inch thick; set it back into the oven until the meringue is well "set." Eat cold.

COCOANUT PIE. No. 1.

One-half cup desiccated cocoanut soaked in one cupful of milk, two eggs, one small cupful of sugar, butter the size of an egg. This is for one small-sized pie. Nice with a meringue on top.

COCOANUT PIE. No. 2.

Cut off the brown part of the cocoanut, grate the white part, mix it with milk and set it on the fire and let it boil slowly eight or ten minutes. To a pound of the grated cocoanut, allow a quart of milk, eight eggs, four tablespoonfuls of sifted white sugar, a glass of wine, a small cracker, pounded fine, two spoonfuls of melted butter and half a nutmeg. The eggs and sugar should be beaten together to a froth, then the wine stirred in. Put them into the milk and cocoanut, which should be first allowed to get quite cool; add the cracker and nutmeg, turn the whole into deep pie plates, with a lining and rim of puff paste. Bake them as soon as turned into the plates.

CHOCOLATE CUSTARD PIE. No. 1.

One-quarter cake of Baker's chocolate, grated; one pint of boiling water, six eggs, one quart of milk, one-half cupful of white sugar, two teaspoonfuls of vanilla. Dissolve the chocolate in a very little milk, stir into the boiling water and boil three minutes. When nearly cold beat up with this the yolks of all the eggs and the whites of three. Stir this mixture into the milk, season and pour into shells of good paste. When the custard is "set"—but not more than half done—spread over it the whites whipped to a froth, with two tablespoonfuls of sugar. You may bake these custards without paste, in a pudding dish or cups set in boiling water.

CHOCOLATE PIE. No. 2.

Put some grated chocolate into a basin and place on the back of the stove and let it melt (do not add any water to it); beat one egg and some sugar in it; when melted, spread this on the top of a custard pie. Lovers of chocolate will like this.

LEMON PIE. No. 1. (Superior.)

Take a deep dish, grate into it the outside of the rind of two lemons; add to that a cup and a half of white sugar, two heaping tablespoonfuls of unsifted flour, or one of cornstarch; stir it well together, then add the yolks of three well-beaten eggs, beat this thoroughly, then add the juice of the lemons, two cups of water and a piece of butter the size of a walnut. Set this on the fire in another dish containing boiling water and cook it until it thickens, and will dip up on the spoon like cold honey. Remove from the fire, and when cooled, pour it into a deep pie-tin, lined with pastry; bake, and when done, have ready the whites, beaten stiff, with three small tablespoonfuls of sugar. Spread this over the top and return to the oven, to set and brown slightly. This makes a deep, large sized pie, and very superior.

Ebbitt House, Washington.

LEMON PIE. No. 2.

One coffee cupful of sugar, three eggs, one cupful of water, one tablespoonful of melted butter, one heaping tablespoonful of flour, the juice and a little of the rind of one lemon. Reserve the whites of the eggs, and after the pie is baked, spread them over the top beaten lightly-with a spoonful of sugar, and return to the oven until it is a light brown.

This may be cooked before it is put into the crust or not, but it is rather better to cook it first in a double boiler or dish. It makes a medium-sized pie. Bake from thirty-five to forty minutes.

LEMON PIE. No. 3.

Moisten a heaping tablespoonful of cornstarch with a little cold water, then add a cupful of boiling water; stir over the fire till it boils and cook the cornstarch, say two or three minutes; add teaspoonful of butter and a cupful of sugar; take off the fire and, when slightly cooled, add an egg well beaten and the juice and grated rind of a fresh lemon. Bake with a crust. This makes one small pie.

LEMON PIE. No. 4.

Two large, fresh lemons, grate off the rind, if not bitter reserve it for the filling of the pie, pare off every bit of the white skin of the lemon (as it toughens while cooking); then cut the lemon into very thin slices with a sharp knife and take out the seeds; two cupfuls of sugar, three tablespoonfuls of water and two of sifted flour. Put into the pie a layer of lemon, then one of sugar, then one of the grated rind and, lastly, of flour, and so on till the ingredients are used; sprinkle the water over all, and cover with upper crust. Be sure to have the under crust lap over the upper, and pinch it well, as the syrup will cook all out if care is not taken when finishing the edge of crust. This quantity makes one medium-sized pie.

ORANGE PIE.

Grate the rind of one and use the juice of two large oranges. Stir together a large cupful of sugar and a heaping tablespoonful of flour; add to this the well-beaten yolks of three eggs, two tablespoonfuls of melted butter. Reserve the whites for frosting. Turn this into a pie-pan lined with pie paste and bake in a quick oven. When done so as to resemble a finely baked custard, spread on the top of it the beaten whites, which must be sweetened with two tablespoonfuls of sugar; spread evenly and return to the oven and brown slightly.

The addition of the juice of half a lemon improves it, if convenient to have it.

BAKERS' CUSTARD PIE.

Beat up the yolks of three eggs to a cream. Stir thoroughly a tablespoonful of sifted flour into three tablespoonfuls of sugar; this separates the particles of flour so that there will be no lumps; then add it to the beaten yolks, put in a pinch of salt, a teaspoonful of vanilla and a little grated nutmeg; next the well-beaten whites of the eggs; and, lastly, a pint of scalded milk (not boiled) which has been cooled; mix this in by degrees and turn all into a deep pie-pan lined with puff paste, and bake from twenty-five to thirty minutes.

I received this recipe from a celebrated cook in one of our best New York bakeries. I inquired of him "why it was that their custard pies had that look of solidity and smoothness that our home-made pies have not." He replied, "The secret is the addition of this *bit of flour*—not that it thickens the custard any to speak of, but prevents the custard from breaking or wheying and gives that smooth appearance when cut."

CREAM PIE.

Pour a pint of cream upon one and a half cupfuls of sugar; let it stand until the whites of three eggs have been beaten to a stiff froth; add this to the cream and beat up thoroughly; grate a little nutmeg over the mixture and bake without an upper crust. If a tablespoonful of sifted flour is added to it, as the above Custard Pie recipe, it would improve it.

WHIPPED CREAM PIE.

Line a pie plate with a rich crust and bake quickly in a hot oven. When done, spread with a thin layer of jelly or jam, then whip one cupful of thick sweet cream until it is as light as possible; sweeten with powdered sugar and flavor with vanilla; spread over the jelly or jam; set the cream where it will get very cold before whipping.

CUSTARD PIE.

Beat together until very light the yolks of four eggs and four tablespoonfuls of sugar, flavor with nutmeg or vanilla; then add the four beaten whites, a pinch of salt and, lastly, a quart of sweet milk; mix well and pour into tins lined with paste. Bake until firm.

BOSTON CREAM PIE.

Cream Part.—Put on a pint of milk to boil. Break two eggs into a dish and add one cup of sugar and half a cup of flour previously mixed after beating well, stir it into the milk just as the milk commences to boil; add an ounce of butter and keep on stirring one way until it thickens; flavor with vanilla or lemon.

Crust Part.—Three eggs beaten separately, one cup of granulated sugar, one and a half cups of sifted flour, one large teaspoonful of baking powder and two tablespoonfuls of milk or water. Divide the batter in half and bake on two medium-sized pie-tins. Bake in a rather quick oven to a straw color. When done and cool, split each one in half with a sharp broad-bladed knife, and spread half the cream between each. Serve cold.

The cake part should be flavored the same as the custard.

MOCK CREAM PIE.

Take three eggs, one pint of milk, a cupful of sugar, two tablespoonfuls of cornstarch or three of flour; beat the sugar, cornstarch and yolks of the eggs together; after the milk has come to a boil, stir in the mixture and add a pinch of salt and about a teaspoonful of butter. Make crust the same as any pie; bake, then fill with the custard, grate over a little nutmeg and bake again. Take the whites of the eggs and beat to a stiff froth with two tablespoonfuls of sugar, spread over the top and brown in a quick oven.

FRUIT CUSTARD PIE.

Any fruit custard, such as pineapple, banana, can be readily made after the recipe of APPLE CUSTARD PIE.

CHERRY PIE.

Line your pie plate with good crust, fill half full with ripe cherries; sprinkle over them about a cupful of sugar, a teaspoonful of sifted flour, dot a few bits of butter over that. Now fill the crust full to the top. Cover with the upper crust and bake.

This is one of the best of pies, if made correctly, and the cherries in any case should be stoned.

CURRANT PIE.

Make in just the same way as the "Cherry Pie," unless they are somewhat green, then they should be stewed a little.

RIPE CURRANT PIE.

One cupful of mashed ripe currants, one of sugar, two tablespoonfuls of water, one of flour, beaten with the yolks of two eggs. Bake; frost the top with the beaten whites of the eggs and two tablespoonfuls powdered sugar and brown in oven.

GREEN TOMATO PIE.

Take medium-sized tomatoes, pare and cut out the stem end. Having your pie-pan lined with paste made as biscuit dough, slice the tomatoes *very thin*, filling the pan somewhat heaping, then grate over it a nutmeg; put in half a cup of butter and a medium cup of sugar, if the pan is rather deep. Sprinkle a small handful of flour over all, pouring in half a cup of vinegar before adding the top crust. Bake half an hour in a moderately hot oven, serving hot. Is good; try it.

APRICOT MERINGUE PIE.

A canned apricot meringue pie is made by cutting the apricots fine and mixing them with half a cup of sugar and the beaten yolk of an egg; fill the crust and bake. Take from the oven, let it stand for two or three minutes, cover with a meringue made of the beaten white of an egg and one tablespoonful of sugar. Set back in a slow oven until it turns a golden brown. The above pie can be made into a tart without the addition of the meringue by adding criss-cross strips of pastry when the pie is first put into the oven.

All of the above are good if made from the dried and stewed apricots instead of the canned and are much cheaper.

Stewed dried apricots are a delicious addition to mince meat. They may be used in connection with minced apples, or to the exclusion of the latter.

HUCKLEBERRY PIE.

Put a quart of picked huckleberries into a basin of water; take off, whatever floats; take up the berries by the handful, pick out all the stems and unripe berries and put them into a dish; line a buttered pie, dish with a pie paste, put in the berries half an inch deep, and to a quart of berries, put half of a teacupful of brown sugar; dredge a teaspoonful of flour over, strew a saltspoonful of salt and a little nutmeg grated over; cover the pie, cut a slit in the centre, or make several small incisions on either side of it; press the two crusts together around the edge, trim it off neatly with a sharp knife and bake in a quick oven for three-quarters of an hour.

BLACKBERRY PIE.

Pick the berries clean, rinse them in cold water and finish as directed for huckleberries.

MOLASSES PIE.

Two teacupfuls of molasses; one of sugar, three eggs, one tablespoonful of melted butter, one lemon, nutmeg; beat and bake in pastry.

LEMON RAISIN PIE.

One cup of chopped raisins, seeded, and the juice and grated rind of one lemon, one cupful of cold water, one tablespoonful of flour, one cupful of sugar, two tablespoonfuls of butter. Stir lightly together and bake with upper and under crust.

RHUBARB PIE.

Cut the large stalks off where the leaves commence, strip off the outside skin, then cut the stalks in pieces half an inch long; line a pie dish with paste rolled rather thicker than a dollar piece, put a layer of the rhubarb nearly an inch deep; to a quart bowl of cut rhubarb put a large teacupful of sugar; strew it over with a saltspoonful of salt and a little nutmeg grated; shake over a little flour; cover with a rich pie crust, cut a slit in the centre, trim off the edge with a sharp knife and bake in a quick oven until the pie loosens from the dish. Rhubarb pies made in this way are altogether superior to those made of the fruit stewed.

RHUBARB PIE. (Cooked.)

Skin the stalks, cut them into small pieces, wash and put them in a stewpan with no more water than what adheres to them; when cooked, mash them fine and put in a small piece of butter; when cool, sweeten to taste; if liked, add a little lemon-peel, cinnamon or nutmeg; line your plate with thin crust, put in the filling, cover with crust and bake in a *quick* oven; sift sugar over it when served.

PINEAPPLE PIE.

A grated pineapple, its weight in sugar, half its weight in butter, one cupful of cream, five eggs; beat the batter to a creamy froth, add the sugar and yolks of the eggs, continue beating till very light; add the cream, the pineapple grated and the whites of the eggs beaten to a stiff froth. Bake with an under crust. Eat cold.

GRAPE PIE.

Pop the pulps out of the skins into one dish and put the skins into another. Then simmer the pulp a little over the fire to soften it; remove it and rub it through a colander to separate it from the seeds. Then put the skins and pulp together and they are ready for pies or for canning or putting in jugs for other use. Fine for pies.

DAMSON OR PLUM PIE.

Stew the damsons whole in water only sufficient to prevent their burning; when tender and while hot, sweeten them with sugar and let them stand until they become cold; then pour them into pie dishes lined with paste, dredge flour upon them, cover them with the same paste, wet and pinch together the edges of the paste, cut a slit in the centre of the cover through which the vapor may escape and bake twenty minutes.

CHOPPING THE MINCEMEAT.

CHOPPING THE MINCEMEAT.

PEACH PIE.

Peel, stone and slice the peaches. Line a pie plate with crust and lay in your fruit, sprinkling sugar liberally over them in proportion to their sweetness. Allow three peach kernels chopped fine to each pie; pour in a very little water and bake with an upper crust, or with cross-bars of paste across the top.

DRIED FRUIT PIES.

Wash the fruit thoroughly, soak over night in water enough to cover. In the morning stew slowly until nearly done in the same water. Sweeten to taste. The crust, both upper and under, should be rolled thin; a thick crust to a fruit pie is undesirable.

RIPE BERRY PIES.

All made the same as "Cherry Pie." Line your pie-tin with crust, fill half full of berries, shake over a tablespoonful of sifted flour (if very juicy) and as much sugar as is necessary to sweeten sufficiently. Now fill up the crust to the top, making quite full. Cover with crust and bake about forty minutes.

Huckleberry and blackberry pies are improved by putting into them a little ginger and cinnamon.

JELLY AND PRESERVED FRUIT PIES.

Preserved fruit requires no baking; hence, always bake the shell and put in the sweetmeats afterwards; you can cover with whipped cream, or bake a top crust shell; the former is preferable for delicacy.

CRANBERRY PIE.

Take fine, sound, ripe cranberries and with a sharp knife split each one until you have a heaping coffeecupful; put them in a vegetable dish or basin; put over them one cupful of white sugar, half a cup of water, a tablespoon *full* of sifted flour; stir it all together and put into your crust. Cover with an upper crust and bake slowly in a moderate oven. You will find this the true way of making a cranberry pie.

Newport Style.

CRANBERRY TART PIE.

After having washed and picked over the berries, stew them well in a little water, just enough to cover them; when they burst open and become soft, sweeten them with plenty of sugar, mash them smooth (some prefer them not mashed); line your pie-plates with thin puff paste, fill them and lay strips of paste across the top. Bake in a moderate oven. Or you may rub them through a colander to free them from the skins.

GOOSEBERRY PIE.

Can be made the same as "Cranberry Tart Pie," or an upper crust can be put on before baking. Serve with boiled custard or a pitcher of good sweet cream.

STEWED PUMPKIN OR SQUASH FOR PIES.

Deep-colored pumpkins are generally the best. Cut a pumpkin or squash in half, take out the seeds, then cut it up in thick slices, pare the outside and cut again in small pieces. Put it into a large pot or saucepan with a very little water; let it cook slowly until tender. Now set the pot on the back of the stove, where it will not burn, and cook slowly, stirring often until the moisture is dried out and the pumpkin looks dark and red. It requires cooking a long time, at least half a day, to have it dry and rich. When cool press through a colander.

BAKED PUMPKIN OR SQUASH FOR PIES.

Cut up in several pieces, do not pare it; place them on baking tins and set them in the oven; bake slowly until soft, then take them out, scrape all the pumpkin from the shell, rub it through a colander. It will be fine and light and free from lumps.

PUMPKIN PIE. No. 1.

For three pies: One quart of milk, three cupfuls of boiled and strained pumpkin, one and one-half cupfuls of sugar, one-half cupful of molasses, the yolks and whites of four eggs beaten separately, a little salt, one tablespoonful each of ginger and cinnamon. Beat all together and bake with an under crust.

Boston marrow or Hubbard squash may be substituted for pumpkin and are much preferred by many, as possessing a less strong flavor.

PUMPKIN PIE. No. 2.

One quart of stewed pumpkin pressed through a sieve, nine eggs, whites and yolks beaten separately, two scant quarts of milk, one teaspoonful of mace, one teaspoonful of cinnamon and the same of nutmeg, one and one-half cupfuls of white sugar, or very light brown. Beat all well together and bake in crust without cover.

A tablespoonful of brandy is a great improvement to pumpkin, or squash pies.

PUMPKIN PIE WITHOUT EGGS.

One quart of properly stewed pumpkin pressed through a colander; to this add enough good, rich milk, sufficient to moisten it enough to fill two good-sized earthen pie-plates, a teaspoonful of salt, half a cupful of molasses or brown sugar, a tablespoonful of ginger, one teaspoonful of cinnamon or nutmeg. Bake in a moderately slow oven three-quarters of an hour.

SQUASH PIE.

One pint of boiled dry squash, one cupful of brown sugar, three eggs, two tablespoonfuls of molasses, one tablespoonful of melted butter one tablespoonful of ginger, one teaspoonful of cinnamon, a pinch of salt and one pint of milk. This makes two pies, or one large deep one.

SWEET POTATO PIE.

One pound of steamed sweet potatoes finely mashed,-two cups sugar, one cup cream, one-half cup butter, three well-beaten eggs, flavor with lemon or nutmeg and bake in pastry shell. Fine.

COOKED MEAT FOR MINCE PIES.

In order to succeed in having good mince pie, it is quite essential to cook the meat properly, so as to retain its juices and strength of flavor.

Select four pounds of lean beef, the neck piece is as good as any; wash it and put it into a kettle with just water enough to cover it; take off the scum as it reaches the boiling point, add hot water from time to time, until it is tender, then season with salt and pepper; take off the cover and let it boil until almost dry, or until the juice has boiled back into the meat. When it looks as though it was beginning to fry in its own juice, it is time to take up and set aside to get cold, which should be done the day before needed. Next day, when making the mince meat, the bones, gristle and stringy bits should be well picked out before chopping.

MINCE PIES. No. 1.

The "Astor House," some years ago, was *famous* for its "mince pies." The chief pastry cook at that time, by request, published the recipe. I find that those who partake of it never fail to speak in laudable terms of the superior excellence of this recipe when strictly followed.

Four pounds of lean boiled beef chopped fine, twice as much of chopped green tart apples, one pound of chopped suet, three pounds of raisins, seeded, two pounds of currants picked over, washed and dried, half a pound of citron, cut up fine, one pound of brown sugar, one quart of cooking molasses, two quarts of sweet cider, one pint of boiled cider, one tablespoonful of salt, one tablespoonful of pepper, one tablespoonful of mace, one tablespoonful of allspice and four tablespoonfuls of cinnamon, two grated nutmegs, one tablespoonful of cloves; mix thoroughly and warm it on the range until heated through. Remove from the fire and when nearly cool, stir in a pint of good brandy and one pint of Madeira wine. Put into a crock, cover it tightly and set it in a cold place where it will not freeze, but keep perfectly cold. Will keep good all winter.

Chef de Cuisine, Astor House, N. Y.

MINCE PIES. No. 2.

Two pounds of lean fresh beef, boiled and, when cold, chopped fine. One pound of beef suet, cleared of strings and minced to powder. Five pounds of apples, pared and chopped, two pounds of raisins, seeded and chopped, one pound of Sultana raisins, washed and picked over, two pounds of currants washed and *carefully* picked over, three-quarters of a pound of citron cut up fine, two tablespoonfuls cinnamon, one of powdered nutmeg, two of mace, one of cloves, one of allspice, one of fine salt, two and a quarter pounds of brown sugar, one quart brown sherry, one pint best brandy.

Mince-meat made by this recipe will keep all winter. Cover closely in a jar and set in a cool place.

Common Sense in the Household.

For preserving mince meat, look for CANNED MINCE MEAT.

MOCK MINCE MEAT WITHOUT MEAT.

One cupful of cold water, half a cupful of molasses, half a cupful of brown sugar, half a cupful of cider vinegar, two-thirds of a cupful of melted butter, one cupful of raisins seeded and chopped, one egg beaten light, half a cupful of rolled cracker crumbs, a teaspoonful of cinnamon, a teaspoonful each of cloves, allspice, nutmeg, salt and black pepper.

Put the saucepan on the fire with the water and raisins; let them cook a few minutes, then add the sugar and molasses, then the vinegar, then the other ingredients; lastly, add a wine-glassful of brandy. Very fine.

FRUIT TURNOVERS. (Suitable for Picnics.)

Make a nice puff paste; roll it out the usual thickness, as for pies; then cut it out into circular pieces about the size of a small tea saucer; pile the fruit on half of the paste, sprinkle over some sugar, wet the edges and turn the paste over. Press the edges together, ornament them and brush the turnovers over with the white of an egg; sprinkle over sifted sugar and bake on tins, in a brisk oven, for about twenty minutes. Instead of putting the fruit in raw, it may be boiled down with a little sugar first and then enclosed in the crust; or jam of any kind may be substituted for fresh fruit.

PLUM CUSTARD TARTLETS.

One pint of greengage plums, after being rubbed through a sieve, one large cup of sugar, the yolks of two eggs well beaten. Whisk all together until light and foamy, then bake in small patty-pans shells of puff paste a light brown. Then fill with the plum paste, beat the two whites until stiff, add two tablespoonfuls of powdered sugar, spread over the plum paste and set the shells into a moderate oven for a few moments.

These are much more easily handled than pieces of pie or even pies whole, and can be packed nicely for carrying.

LEMON TARTLETS. No. 1.

Put a quart of milk into a saucepan over the fire. When it comes to the boiling point put into it the following mixture: Into a bowl put a heaping tablespoonful of flour, half a cupful of sugar and a pinch of salt. Stir this all together thoroughly; then add the beaten yolks of six eggs; stir this one way into the boiling milk until cooked to a thick cream; remove from the fire and stir into it the grated rind and juice of one large lemon. Have ready baked and hot some puff paste tart shells. Fill them with the custard and cover each with a meringue made of the whites of the eggs, sweetened with four tablespoonfuls of sugar. Put into the oven and bake a light straw color.

LEMON TARTLETS. No. 2.

Mix well together the juice and grated rind of two lemons, two cupfuls of sugar, two eggs and the crumbs of sponge cake; beat it all together until smooth; put into twelve patty-pans lined with puff paste and bake until the crust is done.

ORANGE TARTLETS.

Take the juice of two large oranges and the grated peel of one, three-fourths of a cup of sugar, a tablespoonful of butter; stir in a good teaspoonful of cornstarch into the juice of half a lemon and add to the mixture. Beat all well together and bake in tart shells without cover.

MERINGUE CUSTARD TARTLETS.

Select deep individual pie-tins; fluted tartlet pans are suitable for custard tarts, but they should be about six inches in diameter and from two to three inches deep. Butter the pan and line it with ordinary puff paste, then fill it with a custard made as follows: Stir gradually into the beaten yolks of six eggs two tablespoonfuls of flour, a saltspoonful of salt and half a pint of cream. Stir until free from lumps and add two tablespoonfuls of sugar; put the saucepan on the range and stir until the custard coats the spoon. Do not let it boil or it will curdle. Pour it in a bowl, add a few drops of vanilla flavoring and stir until the custard becomes cold; fill the lined mold with this and bake in a moderate oven. In the meantime, put the whites of the eggs in a bright copper vessel and beat thoroughly, using a baker's wire egg-beater for this purpose. While beating, sprinkle in lightly half a pound of sugar and a dash of salt. When the paste is quite firm, spread a thin layer of it over the tart and decorate the top with the remainder by squeezing it through a paper funnel. Strew a little powdered sugar over the top, return to the oven, and when a delicate yellow tinge remove from the oven and when cold serve.

BERRY TARTS.

Line small pie-tins with pie crust and bake. Just before ready to use fill the tarts with strawberries, blackberries, raspberries, or whatever berries are in season. Sprinkle over each tart a little sugar; after adding berries add also to each tart a tablespoonful of sweet cream. They form a delicious addition to the breakfast table.

CREAM STRAWBERRY TARTS.

After picking over the berries carefully, arrange them in layers in a deep pie-tin lined with puff paste, sprinkling sugar thickly between each layer: fill the pie-tin pretty full, pouring in a quantity of the juice: cover with a thick crust, with a slit in the top and bake. When the pie is baked, pour into the slit in the top of the pie the following cream mixture: Take a small cupful of the cream from the top of the morning's milk, heat it until it comes to a boil, then stir into it the whites of two eggs beaten light, also a tablespoonful of white sugar and a teaspoonful of cornstarch wet in cold milk. Boil all together a few moments until quite smooth; set it aside and when cool pour it into the pie through the slit in the crust. Serve it cold with powdered sugar sifted over it.

Raspberry, blackberry and whortleberry may be made the same.

GREEN GOOSEBERRY TART.

Top and tail the gooseberries. Put into a porcelain kettle with enough water to prevent burning and stew slowly until they break. Take them off, sweeten *well* and set aside to cool. When cold pour into pastry shells and bake with a top crust of puff paste. Brush all over with beaten egg while hot, set back in the oven to glaze for three minutes. Eat cold.

Common Sense in the Household.

COCOANUT TARTS.

Take three cocoanuts, the meats grated, the yolks of five eggs, half a cupful of white sugar, season, a wine-glass of milk; put the butter in cold and bake in a nice puff paste.

CHOCOLATE TARTS.

Four eggs, whites and yolks, one-half cake of Baker's chocolate, grated, one tablespoonful of cornstarch, dissolved in water, three tablespoonfuls of milk, four of white sugar, two teaspoonfuls of vanilla, one saltspoonful of salt, one-half teaspoonful of cinnamon, one teaspoonful of butter, melted; rub the chocolate smooth in the milk and heat to boiling over the fire, then stir in the cornstarch. Stir five minutes until well thickened, remove from the fire and pour into a bowl. Beat all the yolks and the whites of two eggs well with the sugar, and when the chocolate mixture is almost cold, put all together with the flavoring and stir until light. Bake in open shells of pastry. When done, cover with a meringue made of the whites of two eggs and two tablespoonfuls of sugar flavored with a teaspoonful of lemon juice. Eat cold.

These are nice for tea, baked in patty-pans.

Common Sense in the Household.

MAIDS OF HONOR.

Take one cupful of sour milk, one of sweet milk, a tablespoonful of melted butter, the yolks of four eggs, juice and rind of one lemon and a small cupful of white pounded sugar. Put both kinds of milk together in a vessel, which is set in another and let it become sufficiently heated to set the curd, then strain off the milk, rub the curd through a strainer, add butter to the curd, the sugar, well-beaten eggs and lemon. Line the little pans with the richest of puff paste and fill with the mixture; bake until firm in the centre, from ten to fifteen minutes.

GERMAN FRUIT PIE.

Sift together a heaping teaspoonful of baking powder and a pint of flour; add a piece of butter as large as a walnut, a pinch of salt, one beaten egg and sweet milk enough to make a soft dough. Roll it out half an inch thick;

butter a square biscuit tin and cover the bottom and sides with the dough; fill the pan with quartered juicy apples, sprinkle with a little cinnamon and molasses. Bake in rather quick oven until the crust and apples are cooked a light brown. Sprinkle a little sugar over the top five minutes before removing from the oven.

Ripe peaches are fine used in the same manner.

APPLE TARTS.

Pare, quarter, core and boil in half a cupful of water, until quite soft, ten large, tart apples; beat until very smooth and add the yolks of six eggs, or three whole ones, the juice and grated outside rind of two lemons, half a cap of butter; one and a half of sugar (or more, if not sufficiently sweet); beat all thoroughly, line patty-pans with a puff paste and fill; bake five minutes in a hot oven.

Meringue.—If desired very nice, cover them when removed from the oven with the meringue made of the whites of three eggs remaining, mixed with three tablespoonfuls of sugar; return to the oven and delicately brown.

CREAM TARTS.

Make a rich, brittle crust, with which cover your patty-pans, smoothing off the edges nicely and bake well. While these "shells" are cooling, take one teacupful (more or less according to the number of tarts you want) of perfectly sweet and fresh cream, skimmed free of milk; put this into a large bowl or other deep dish, and with your egg-beater whip it to a thick, stiff froth; add a heaping tablespoonful of fine white sugar, with a teaspoonful (a small one) of lemon or vanilla. Fill the cold shells with this and set in a cool place till tea is ready.

OPEN JAM TARTS.

Time to bake until paste loosens from the dish. Line shallow tin dish with puff paste, put in the jam, roll out some of the paste, wet it lightly with the yolk of an egg beaten with a little milk, and a tablespoonful of powdered sugar. Cut it in narrow strips, then lay them across the tart, lay another strip around the edge, trim off outside, and bake in a quick oven.

CHESS CAKES.

Peel and grate one cocoanut; boil one pound of sugar fifteen minutes in two-thirds of a pint of water; stir in the grated cocoanut and boil fifteen minutes longer. While warm, stir in a quarter of a pound of butter; add the yolks of seven eggs well beaten. Bake in patty-pans with rich paste. If prepared cocoanut is used, take one and a half coffeecupfuls. Fine.

CUSTARDS, CREAMS AND DESSERTS.

The usual rule for custards is, eight eggs to a quart of milk; but a very good custard can be made of six, or even less, especially with the addition of a level tablespoonful of sifted flour, thoroughly blended in the sugar first, before adding the other ingredients. They may be baked, boiled or steamed, either in cups or one large dish. It improves custard to first boil the milk and then cool it before being used; also a little salt adds to the flavor. A very small lump of butter may also be added, if one wants something especially rich.

To make custards look and taste better, duck's eggs should be used when obtainable; they add very much to the flavor and richness, and so many are not required as of ordinary eggs, four duck's eggs to the pint of milk making a delicious custard. When desired extremely rich and good, cream should be substituted for the milk, and double the quantity of eggs used to those mentioned, omitting the whites.

When making boiled custard, set the dish containing the custard into another and larger dish, partly filled with boiling water, placed over the fire. Let the cream or milk come almost to a boil before adding the eggs or thickening, then stir it briskly one way every moment until smooth and well cooked; it must *not* boil or it will curdle.

To bake a custard, the fire should be moderate and the dish well buttered.

Everything in baked custard depends upon the *regularly heated slow* oven. If made with nicety it is the most delicate of all sweets; if cooked till it wheys it is hardly eatable.

Frozen eggs can be made quite as good as fresh ones if used as soon as thawed soft. Drop them into boiling water, letting them remain until the water is cold. They will be soft all through and beat up equal to those that have not been touched with the frost.

Eggs should always be thoroughly well beaten separately, the yolks first, then the sugar added, beat again, then add the beaten whites with the flavoring, then the cooled scalded milk. The lighter the eggs are beaten, the thicker and richer the custard.

Eggs should always be broken into a cup, the whites and yolks separated, and they should always be strained. Breaking the eggs thus, the bad ones may be easily rejected without spoiling the others and so cause no waste.

A meringue, or frosting for the top, requires about a tablespoonful of fine sugar to the beaten white of one egg; to be placed on the top after the custard or pudding is baked, smoothed over with a broad-bladed knife dipped in cold water, and replaced in the oven to brown slightly.

SOFT CARAMEL CUSTARD.

One quart of milk, half a cupful of sugar, six eggs, half a teaspoonful of salt. Put the milk on to boil, reserving a cupful. Beat the eggs and add the cold milk to them. Stir the sugar in a small frying pan until it becomes liquid and just begins to smoke. Stir it into the boiling milk; then add the beaten eggs and cold milk and stir constantly until the mixture begins to thicken. Set away to cool. Serve in glasses.

BAKED CUSTARD.

Beat five fresh eggs, the whites and yolks separately, the yolks with half a cup of sugar, the whites to a stiff froth; then stir them gradually into a quart of sweet rich milk previously boiled and cooled; flavor with extract of lemon or vanilla and half a teaspoonful of salt. Rub butter over the bottom and sides of a baking-dish or tin basin; pour in the custard, grate a little nutmeg over and bake in a quick oven. It is better to set the dish in a shallow pan of hot water reaching nearly to the top, the water to be kept boiling until the custard is baked; three-quarters of an hour is generally enough. Run a teaspoon handle into the middle of it; if it comes out clean it is baked sufficiently.

CUP CUSTARD.

Six eggs half a cupful of sugar, one quart of new milk. Beat the eggs and the sugar and milk, and any extract or flavoring you like. Fill your custard cups, sift a little nutmeg or cinnamon over the tops, set them in a moderate oven in a shallow pan half filled with hot water. In about twenty minutes try them with the handle of a teaspoon to see if they are firm. Judgment and great care are needed to attain skill in baking custard, for if left in the oven a minute too long, or if the fire is too hot, the milk will certainly whey.

Serve cold with fresh fruit sugared and placed on top of each. Strawberries, peaches or raspberries, as preferred.

BOILED CUSTARD.

Beat seven eggs very light, omitting the whites of two; mix them gradually with a quart of milk and half a cupful of sugar; boil in a dish set in another of boiling water; add flavoring. As soon as it comes to the boiling point remove it, or it will be liable to curdle and become lumpy. Whip the whites of the two eggs that remain, adding two heaping tablespoonfuls of sugar. When the custard is cold heap this on top; if in cups, put on a strawberry or a bit of red jelly on each. Set in a cold place till wanted.

Common Sense in the Household.

BOILED CUSTARD, OR MOCK CREAM.

Take two even tablespoonfuls of cornstarch, one quart of milk, three eggs, half a teaspoonful of salt and a small piece of butter; heat the milk to nearly boiling and add the starch, previously dissolved in a little cold milk; then add the eggs well beaten with four tablespoonfuls of powdered sugar; let it boil up once or twice, stirring it briskly, and it is done. Flavor with lemon, or vanilla, or raspberry, or to suit your taste.

A good substitute for ice cream, served *very* cold.

FRENCH CUSTARD.

One quart of milk, eight eggs, sugar and cinnamon to taste; separate the eggs, beat the yolks until thick, to which add the milk, a little vanilla, and sweeten to taste; put it into a pan or farina kettle, place it over a slow fire and stir it all the time until it becomes custard; then pour it into a pudding-dish to get cold; whisk the whites until stiff and dry; have ready a pan of boiling water on the top of which place the whites; cover and place them where the water will keep sufficiently hot to cause a steam to pass through and cook them; place in a dish (suitable for the table) a layer of custard and white alternately; on each layer of custard grate a little nutmeg with a teaspoonful of wine; reserve a layer of white for the cover, over which grate nutmeg; then send to table and eat cold.

GERMAN CUSTARD.

Add to a pint of good, rich, boiled custard an ounce of sweet almonds, blanched, roasted and pounded to a paste, and half an ounce of pine-nuts or peanuts, blanched, roasted and pounded; also a small quantity of candied citron cut into the thinnest possible slips; cook the custard as usual and set it on the ice for some hours before using.

APPLE CUSTARD.

Pare, core and quarter a dozen large juicy pippins. Stew among them the yellow peel of a large lemon grated very fine, and stew them till tender in a very small portion of water. When done, mash them smooth with the back of a spoon (you must have a pint and a half of the stewed apple); mix a half cupful of sugar with them and set them away till cold. Beat six eggs very light and stir them gradually into a quart of rich milk alternately with the stewed apple. Put the mixture into cups, or into a deep dish and bake it about twenty minutes. Send it to table cold, with nutmeg grated over the top.

ALMOND CUSTARD. No. 1.

Scald and blanch half a pound of shelled sweet almonds and three ounces of bitter almonds, throwing them, as you do them, into a large bowl of cold water. Then pound them one at a time into a paste, adding a few drops of wine or rose-water to them. Beat eight eggs very light with two-thirds of a cup of sugar, then mix together with a quart of rich milk, or part milk and part cream; put the mixture into a saucepan and set it over the fire. Stir it one way until it begins to thicken, but not till it curdles; remove from the fire and when it is cooled put in a glass dish. Having reserved part of the whites of the eggs, beat them to a stiff froth, season with three tablespoonfuls of sugar and a teaspoonful of lemon extract, spread over the top of the custard. Serve cold.

ALMOND CUSTARD. No. 2.

Blanch a quarter of a pound of sweet almonds, pound them, as in No. 1 on preceding page, with six ounces of fine white sugar and mix them well with the yolks of four eggs; then dissolve one ounce of patent gelatine in one quart of boiling milk, strain it through a sieve and pour into it the other mixture; stir the whole over the fire until it thickens and is smooth; then pour it into your mold and keep it upon ice, or in a cool place, until wanted; when ready to serve dip the mold into warm water, rub it with a cloth and turn out the cream carefully upon your dish.

SNOWBALL CUSTARD.

Soak half a package of Cox's gelatine in a teacupful of cold water one hour, to which add a pint of boiling water, stir it until the gelatine is thoroughly dissolved. Then beat the whites of four eggs to a stiff froth, put two teacupfuls of sugar in the gelatine water first, then the beaten white of egg and one teaspoonful of vanilla extract, or the grated rind and the juice of a lemon. Whip it some time until it is all quite stiff and cold. Dip some teacups or wine-glasses in cold water and fill them; set in a cold place.

In the meantime, make a boiled custard of the yolks of three of the eggs, with half a cupful of sugar and a pint of milk; flavor with vanilla extract. Now after the meringue in the cups has stood four or five hours, turn them out of the molds, place them in a glass dish and pour this custard around the base.

BAKED COCOANUT CUSTARD.

Grate as much cocoanut as will weigh a pound. Mix half a pound of powdered white sugar with the milk of the cocoanut, or with a pint of cream, adding two tablespoonfuls of rose-water. Then stir in gradually a pint of rich milk. Beat to a stiff froth the whites of eight eggs and stir them into the milk and sugar, a little at a time, alternately with the grated cocoanut; add a teaspoonful of powdered nutmeg and cinnamon. Then put the mixture into cups and bake them twenty minutes in a moderate oven, set in a pan half filled with boiling water. When cold, grate loaf sugar over them.

WHIPPED CREAM. No. 1.

To the whites of three eggs, beaten to a stiff froth, add a pint of thick sweet cream (previously set where it is very cold) and four tablespoonfuls of sweet wine, with three of fine white sugar and a teaspoonful of the extract of lemon or vanilla. Mix all the ingredients together on a board platter or pan and whip it to a standing froth; as the froth rises, take it off lightly with a spoon and lay it on an inverted sieve with a dish under it to catch what will drain through; and what drains through can be beaten over again.

Serve in a glass dish with jelly or jam and sliced sponge cake. This should be whipped in a cool place and set in the ice box.

WHIPPED CREAM. No. 2.

Three coffeecupfuls of good thick sweet cream, half a cup of powdered sugar, three teaspoonfuls of vanilla; whip it to a stiff froth. Dissolve three-fourths of an ounce of best gelatine in a teacup of hot water and when cool pour it in the cream and stir it gently from the bottom upward, cutting the cream into it, until it thickens. The dish which contains the cream should be set in another dish containing ice-water, or cracked ice. When finished pour in molds and set on ice or in any very cold place.

SPANISH CREAM.

Take one quart of milk and soak half a box of gelatine in it for an hour; place it on the fire and stir often. Beat the yolks of three eggs very light with a cupful of sugar, stir into the scalding milk and heat until it begins to thicken (it should not boil, or it will curdle); remove from the fire and strain through thin muslin or tarlatan, and when nearly cold flavor with vanilla or lemon; then wet a dish or mold in cold water and set aside to stiffen.

BAVARIAN CREAM.

One quart of sweet cream, the yolks of four eggs beaten together with a cupful of sugar. Dissolve half an ounce of gelatine or isinglass in half a teacupful of warm water; when it is dissolved stir in a pint of boiling hot cream; add the beaten yolks and sugar; cook all together until it begins to thicken, then remove from the fire and add the other pint of cold cream whipped to a stiff froth, adding a little at a time and beating hard. Season with vanilla or lemon. Whip the whites of the eggs for the top. Dip the mold in cold water before filling; set it in a cold place. To this could be added almonds, pounded, grated chocolate, peaches, pineapples, strawberries, raspberries, or any seasonable fruit.

STRAWBERRY BAVARIAN CREAM.

Pick off the hulls of a box of strawberries, bruise them in a basin with a cup of powered sugar; rub this through a sieve and mix with it a pint of whipped cream and one ounce and a half of clarified isinglass or gelatine; pour the cream into a mold previously oiled. Let it in rough ice and when it has become firm turn out on a dish.

Raspberries or currants may be substituted for strawberries.

GOLDEN CREAM.

Boil a quart of milk; when boiling stir into it the well-beaten yolks of six eggs; add six tablespoonfuls of sugar and one tablespoonful of sifted flour, which have been well beaten together; when boiled, turn it into a dish, and pour over it the whites beaten to a stiff froth, mixing with them six tablespoonfuls, of powdered sugar. Set all in the oven and brown slightly. Flavor the top with vanilla and the bottom with lemon. Serve cold.

CHOCOLATE CREAM. No. 1.

Three ounces of grated chocolate, one-quarter pound of sugar, one and one-half pints of cream, one and one-half ounces of clarified isinglass, or gelatine, the yolks of six eggs.

Beat the yolks of the eggs well; put them into a basin with the grated chocolate, the sugar and one pint of the cream; stir these ingredients well together, pour them into a basin and set this basin in a saucepan of boiling water; stir it one way until the mixture thickens, but *do not allow it to boil*, or it will curdle. Strain the cream through a sieve into a basin, stir in the isinglass and the other one-half pint of cream, which should-be well whipped; mix all well together, and pour it into a mold which has been previously oiled with the purest salad oil, and, if at hand, set it in ice until wanted for table.

MRS ULYSSES S. GRANT, LUCY WEBB HAYES, MRS ANDREW JOHNSON

CHOCOLATE CREAM OR CUSTARD. No. 2.

Take one quart of milk, and when nearly boiling stir in two ounces of grated chocolate; let it warm on the fire for a few moments, and then remove and cool; beat the yolks of eight eggs and two whites with eight tablespoonfuls of sugar, then pour the milk over them; flavor and bake as any custard, either in cups or a large dish. Make a meringue of the remaining whites.

LEMON CREAM. No. 1.

One pint of cream, the yolks of two eggs, one quarter of a pound of white sugar, one large lemon, one ounce isinglass or gelatine.

Put the cream into a *lined* saucepan with the sugar, lemon peel and isinglass, and simmer these over a gentle fire for about ten minutes, stirring them all the time. Strain the cream into a basin, add the yolks of eggs, which should be well beaten, and put the basin into a saucepan of boiling water; stir the mixture one way until it thickens, *but do not allow it to boil*; take it off the fire and keep stirring it until nearly cold. Strain the lemon juice into a basin, gradually pour on it the cream, and *stir it well* until the juice is well mixed with it. Have ready a well-oiled mold, pour the cream into it, and let it remain until perfectly set. When required for table, loosen the edges with a small blunt knife, put a dish on the top of the mold, turn it over quickly, and the cream should easily slip away.

LEMON CREAM. No. 2.

Pare into one quart of boiling water the peels of four large lemons, the yellow outside only; let it stand for four hours; then take them out and add to the water the juice of the four lemons and one cupful of fine white sugar. Beat the yolks of ten eggs and mix all together; strain it through a piece of lawn or lace into a porcelain lined stewpan; set it over a slow fire; stir it one way until it is as thick as good cream, *but do not let it boil*; then take it from the fire, and, when cool, serve in custard cups.

LEMON CREAM. No. 3.

Peel three lemons and squeeze out the juice into one quart of milk. Add the peel; cut in pieces and cover the mixture for a few hours; then add six eggs, well beaten, and one pint of water, well sweetened. Strain and simmer over a gentle fire till it thickens; *do not let it boil.* Serve very cold.

ORANGE CREAM.

Whip a pint of cream so long that there will be but one-half the quantity left when skimmed off. Soak in half a cupful of cold water a half package of gelatine and then grate over it the rind of two oranges. Strain the juice of six oranges and add to it a cupful of sugar; now put the half pint of unwhipped cream into a double boiler, pour into it the well-beaten yolks of six eggs, stirring until it begins to thicken, then add the gelatine. Remove from the fire, let it stand for two minutes and add the orange juice and sugar; beat all together until about the consistency of soft custard and add the whipped cream. Mix well and turn into molds to harden. To be served with sweetened cream. Fine.

SOLID CREAM.

Four tablespoonfuls of pounded sugar, one quart of cream, two tablespoonfuls of brandy, the juice of one large lemon.

Strain the lemon juice over the sugar and add the brandy, then stir in the cream, put the mixture into a pitcher and continue pouring from one pitcher to another, until it is quite thick; or it may be whisked until the desired consistency is obtained. It should be served in jelly glasses.

BANANA CREAM.

After peeling the bananas, mash them with an iron or wooden spoon; allow equal quantities of bananas and sweet cream; to one quart of the mixture, allow one-quarter of a pound of sugar. Beat them all together until the cream is light.

TAPIOCA CREAM CUSTARD.

Soak three heaping tablespoonfuls of tapioca in a teacupful of water over night. Place over the fire a quart of milk; let it come to a boil, then stir in the tapioca, a good pinch of salt, stir until it thickens; then add a cupful of sugar and the beaten yolks of three eggs. Stir it quickly and pour it into a dish and stir gently into the mixture the whites beaten stiff, the flavoring and set it on ice, or in an ice chest.

PEACH CREAM. No. 1.

Mash very smooth two cupfuls of canned peaches, run them through a sieve and cook for three minutes in a syrup made by boiling together one cupful of sugar and stirring all the time. Place the pan containing the syrup and peaches into another of boiling water and add one-half packet of gelatine prepared the same as in previous recipes, and stir for five minutes to thoroughly dissolve the gelatine, then take it from the fire, place in a pan of ice-water, beat until nearly cool and then add the well-frothed whites of six eggs. Beat this whole mixture until it commences to harden. Then pour into a mold, set away to cool and serve with cream and sugar. It should be placed on the ice to cool for two or three hours before serving.

PEACH CREAM. No. 2.

A quart of fine peaches, pare and stone the fruit and cut in quarters. Beat the whites of three eggs with a half cupful of powdered sugar until it is stiff enough to cut with a knife. Take the yolks and mix with half a cupful of granulated sugar and a pint of milk. Put the peaches into the mixture, place in a pudding-dish and bake until almost firm; then put in the whites, mixing all thoroughly again, and bake a light brown. Eat ice cold.

ITALIAN CREAM.

Put two pints of cream into two bowls; with one bowl mix six ounces of powdered loaf sugar, the juice of two large lemons and two glassfuls of white wine; then add the other pint of cream and stir the whole very hard; boil two ounces of isinglass or gelatine with four small teacupfuls of water till reduced to one-half; then stir the mixture luke-warm into the other ingredients; put them in a glass dish to congeal.

SNOW CREAM.

Heat a quart of thick, sweet cream; when ready to boil, stir into it quickly three tablespoonfuls of cornstarch flour, blended with some cold cream; sweeten to taste and allow it to boil gently, stirring for two or three minutes; add quickly the whites of six eggs, beaten to a stiff froth; do not allow it to boil up more than once after adding the eggs; flavor with lemon, vanilla, bitter almond or grated lemon peel; lay the snow thus formed quickly in rocky heaps on silver or glass dishes, or in shapes. Iced, it will turn out well.

If the recipe is closely followed, any family may enjoy it at a trifling expense, and it is really worthy the table of an epicure. It can be made the day before it is to be eaten; kept cold.

MOCK ICE.

Take about three tablespoonfuls of some good preserve; rub it through a sieve with as much cream as will fill a quart mold; dissolve three-quarters of an ounce of isinglass or gelatine in half a pint of water; when almost cold, mix it well with the cream; put it into a mold, set in a cool place and turn out next day.

PEACH MERINGUE.

Pare and quarter (removing stones) a quart of sound, ripe peaches; place them all in a dish that it will not injure to set in the oven and yet be suitable to place on the table. Sprinkle the peaches with sugar, and cover them well with the beaten whites of three eggs. Stand the dish in the oven until the eggs have become a delicate brown, then remove, and when cool enough, set the dish on ice, or in a very cool place. Take the yolks of the eggs, add to them a pint of milk, sweeten and flavor, and boil same in a custard kettle, being careful to keep the eggs from curdling. When cool pour into a glass pitcher and serve with the meringue when ready to use.

APPLE FLOAT.

One dozen apples, pared and cored, one pound and a half of sugar. Put the apples on with water enough to cover them and let them stew until they look as if they would break; then take them out and put the sugar in the same water; let the syrup come to a boil, put in the apples and let them stew until done through and clear; then take them out, slice into the syrup one large lemon and add an ounce of gelatine dissolved in a pint of cold water. Let the whole mix well and come to a boil; then pour upon the apples. The syrup will congeal. It is to be eaten cold with cream.

Or you may change the dish by making a soft custard with the yolks of four eggs, three tablespoonfuls of powdered sugar and a scant quart of milk. When cold, spread it over the apples. Whip the whites of the egg, flavor with lemon and place on the custard. Color in the oven.

SYLLABUB.

One quart of rich milk or cream, a cupful of wine, half a cupful of sugar; put the sugar and wine into a bowl and the milk lukewarm in a separate vessel. When the sugar is dissolved in the wine, pour the milk in, holding it high; pour it back and forth until it is frothy. Grate nutmeg over it.

CREAM FOR FRUIT.

This recipe is an excellent substitute for pure cream, to be eaten on fresh berries and fruit.

One cupful of sweet milk; heat it until boiling. Beat together the whites of two eggs, a tablespoonful of white sugar and a piece of butter the size of a nutmeg. Now add half a cupful of cold milk and a teaspoonful of cornstarch; stir well together until very light and smooth, then add it to the boiling milk; cook it until it thickens; it must not boil. Set it aside to cool. It should be of the consistency of real fresh cream. Serve in a creamer.

STRAWBERRY SPONGE.

One quart of strawberries, half a package of gelatine, one cupful and a half of water, one cupful of sugar, the juice of a lemon, the whites of four eggs. Soak the gelatine for two hours in half a cupful of the water. Mash the strawberries and add half the sugar to them. Boil the remainder of the sugar and the water gently twenty minutes. Rub the strawberries through a sieve. Add the gelatine to the boiling syrup and take from the fire immediately; then add the strawberries. Place in a pan of ice-water and beat five minutes. Add the whites of eggs and beat until the mixture begins to thicken. Pour in the molds and set away to harden. Serve with sugar and cream. Raspberry and blackberry sponges are made in the same way.

LEMON SPONGE.

Lemon sponge is made from the juice of four lemons, four eggs, a cupful of sugar, half a package of gelatine and one pint of water. Strain lemon juice on the sugar; beat the yolks of the eggs and mix with the remainder of the water, having used a half cupful of the pint in which to soak the gelatine. Add the sugar and lemon to this and cook until it begins to thicken, then add the gelatine. Strain this into a basin, which place in a pan of water to cool. Beat with a whisk until it has cooled but not hardened; now add the whites of the eggs until it begins to thicken, turn in a mold and set to harden.

Remember the sponge hardens very rapidly when it commences to cool, so have your molds all ready. Serve with powdered sugar and cream.

APPLE SNOW.

Stew some fine-flavored sour apples tender, sweeten to taste, strain them through a fine wire sieve and break into one pint of strained apples the white of an egg; whisk the apple and egg very briskly till quite stiff and it will be as white as snow; eaten with a nice boiled custard it makes a very desirable dessert. More eggs may be used if liked.

QUINCE SNOW.

Quarter five fair-looking quinces and boil them till they are tender in water, then peel them and push them through a coarse sieve. Sweeten to the taste and add the whites of three or four eggs. Then with an egg-whisk beat all to a stiff froth and pile with a spoon upon a glass dish and set away in the ice box, unless it is to be served immediately.

ORANGE TRIFLE.

Take the thin parings from the outside of a dozen oranges and put to steep in a wide-mouthed bottle; cover it with good cognac and let it stand twenty-four hours; skin and seed the oranges and reduce to a pulp; press this through a sieve, sugar to taste, arrange in a dish and heap with whipped cream flavored with the orange brandy, ice two hours before serving.

LEMON TRIFLE.

The juice of two lemons and grated peel of one, one pint of cream, well sweetened and whipped stiff, one cupful of sherry, a little nutmeg. Let sugar, lemon juice and peel lie together two hours before you add wine and nutmeg. Strain through double tarlatan and whip gradually into the frothed cream. Serve very soon heaped in small glasses. Nice with cake.

FRUIT TRIFLE.

Whites of four eggs beaten to a stiff froth, two tablespoonfuls each of sugar, currant jelly and raspberry jam. Eaten with sponge cakes, it is a delicious dessert.

GRAPE TRIFLE.

Pulp through a sieve two pounds of ripe grapes, enough to keep back the stones, add sugar to taste. Put into a trifle dish and cover > with whipped cream, nicely flavored. Serve very cold.

APPLE TRIFLE.

Peel, core and quarter some good tart apples of nice flavor, and stew them with a strip of orange and a strip of quince peel, sufficient water to cover the bottom of the stewpan, and sugar in the proportion of half a pound to one pound of fruit; when cooked, press the pulp through a sieve, and, when cold, dish and cover with one pint of whipped cream flavored with lemon peel.

Quinces prepared in the same manner are equally as good.

PEACH TRIFLE.

Select perfect, fresh peaches, peel and core and cut in quarters; they should be *well sugared*, arranged in a trifle dish with a few of their own blanched kernels among them, then heaped with whipped cream as above; the cream should not be flavored; this trifle should be set on the ice for at least an hour before serving; home-made sponge cakes should be served with it.

GOOSEBERRY TRIFLE.

One quart of gooseberries, sugar to taste, one pint of custard, a plateful of whipped cream.

Put the gooseberries into a jar, with sufficient moist sugar to sweeten them, and boil them until reduced to a pulp. Put this pulp at the bottom of a trifle dish; pour over it a pint of custard, and, when cold, cover with whipped cream. The cream should be whipped the day before it is wanted for table, as it will then be so much firmer and more solid. This dish may be garnished as fancy dictates.

LEMON HONEY.

One coffeecupful of white sugar, the grated rind and juice of one large lemon, the yolks of three eggs and the white of one, a tablespoonful of butter. Put into a basin the sugar and butter, set it in a dish of boiling water over the fire; while this is melting, beat up the eggs, and add to them the grated rind from the outside of the lemon; then add this to the sugar and butter, cooking and stirring it until it is thick and clear like honey.

This will keep for some days, put into a tight preserve jar, and is nice for flavoring pies, etc.

FLOATING ISLANDS.

Beat the yolks of five eggs and the whites of two very light, sweeten with five tablespoonfuls of sugar and flavor to taste; stir them into a quart of scalded milk and cook it until it thickens. When cool pour it into a glass dish. Now whip the whites of the three remaining eggs to a *stiff* froth, adding three tablespoonfuls of sugar and a little flavoring. Pour this froth over a shallow dish of boiling water; the steam passing through it cooks it; when sufficiently cooked, take a tablespoon and drop spoonfuls of this over the top of the custard, far enough apart so that the "little white islands" will not touch each other. By dropping a teaspoonful of bright jelly on the top or centre of each island, is produced a pleasing effect; also by filling wine-glasses and arranging them around a standard adds much to the appearance of the table.

FLOATING ISLAND.

One quart of milk, five eggs and five tablespoonfuls of sugar. Scald the milk, then add the beaten yolks and one of the whites together with the sugar. First stir into them a little of the scalded milk to prevent curdling, then all of the milk. Cook it the proper thickness; remove from the fire, and, when cool, flavor; then pour it into a glass dish and let it become very cold. Before it is served beat up the remaining four whites of the eggs to a *stiff* froth and beat into them three tablespoonfuls of sugar and two tablespoonfuls of currant jelly. Dip this over the top of the custard.

TAPIOCA BLANC MANGE.

Half a pound of tapioca soaked an hour in one pint of milk and boiled till tender; add a pinch of salt, sweeten to taste and put into a mold; when cold turn it out and serve with strawberry or raspberry jam around it and a little cream. Flavor with lemon or vanilla.

BLANC MANGE. No. 1.

In one teacupful of water boil until dissolved one ounce of clarified isinglass, or of patent gelatine (which is better); stir it continually, while boiling. Then squeeze the juice of a lemon upon a cupful of fine, white sugar; stir the sugar into a quart of rich cream and half a pint of Madeira or sherry wine; when it is well mixed, add the dissolved isinglass or gelatine, stir all well together, pour it into molds previously wet with cold water; set the molds upon ice, let them stand until their contents are hard and cold, then serve with sugar and cream or custard sauce.

BLANC MANGE. No. 2.

Dissolve two ounces of patent gelatine in cold water; when it is dissolved stir it into two quarts of rich milk, with a teacupful of fine white sugar; season it to your taste with lemon, or vanilla, or peach water; place it over the fire and boil it, stirring it continually; let it boil five minutes; then strain it through a cloth, pour it into molds previously wet with cold water and salt; let it stand on ice, or in any cool place until it becomes hard and cold; turn it out carefully upon dishes and serve; or, half fill your mold; when this has set, cover with cherries, peaches in halves, strawberries or sliced bananas, and add the remainder.

CHOCOLATE BLANC MANGE.

Half a box of gelatine soaked in a cupful of water for an hour, half a cupful of grated chocolate, rubbed smooth in a little milk. Boil two cupfuls of milk, then add the gelatine and chocolate and one cupful of sugar; boil all together eight or ten minutes. Remove from the fire, and when nearly cold beat into this the whipped whites of three eggs, flavored with vanilla. Should be served cold with custard made of the yolks, or sugar and cream. Set the molds in a cold place.

CORNSTARCH BLANC MANGE.

Take one quart of sweet milk and put one pint upon the stove to heat; in the other pint mix four heaping tablespoonfuls of cornstarch and half a cupful of sugar; when the milk is hot, pour in the cold milk with the cornstarch and sugar thoroughly mixed in it and stir altogether until there are no lumps and it is thick; flavor with lemon; take from the stove and add the whites of three eggs beaten to a stiff froth.

A Custard for the above.—One pint of milk boiled with a little salt in it; beat the yolks of three eggs with half a cupful of sugar and add to the boiling milk; stir well, but do not let it boil until the eggs are put in; flavor to taste.

FRUIT BLANC MANGE.

Stew nice, fresh fruit (cherries, raspberries and strawberries being the best), or canned ones will do; strain off the juice and sweeten to taste; place it over the fire in a double kettle until it boils; while boiling, stir in cornstarch wet with a little cold water, allowing two tablespoonfuls of cornstarch to each pint of juice; continue stirring until sufficiently cooked; then pour into molds wet in cold water and set away to cool. Served with cream and sugar.

ORANGE CHARLOTTE.

For two molds of medium size, soak half a box of gelatine in half a cupful of water for two hours. Add one and a half cupfuls of boiling water and strain. Then add two cupfuls of sugar, one of orange juice and pulp and the juice of one lemon. Stir until the mixture begins to cool, or about five minutes; then add the whites of six eggs, beaten to a stiff froth. Beat the whole until so stiff that it will only just pour into molds lined with sections of orange. Set away to cool.

STRAWBERRY CHARLOTTE.

Make a boiled custard of one quart of milk, the yolks of six eggs and three-quarters of a cupful of sugar; flavor to taste. Line a glass fruit-dish with slices of sponge cake dipped in sweet cream; lay upon this ripe strawberries sweetened to taste; then a layer of cake and strawberries as before. When the custard is cold pour over the whole. Now beat the whites of the eggs to a stiff froth, add a tablespoonful of sugar to each egg and put over the top. Decorate the top with the largest berries saved out at the commencement.

Raspberry charlotte may be made the same way.

CHARLOTTE RUSSE. (Fine.)

Whip one quart of rich cream to a stiff froth and drain well on a nice sieve. To one scant pint of milk add six eggs beaten very light; make very sweet; flavor high with vanilla. Cook over hot water till it is a thick custard. Soak one full ounce of Cox's gelatine in a very little water and warm over hot water. When the custard is very cold beat in lightly the gelatine and the whipped cream. Line the bottom of your mold with buttered paper, the side with sponge cake or lady-fingers fastened together with the white of an egg.

Fill with the cream, put in a cold place, or, in summer, on ice. To turn out, dip the mold for a moment in hot water. In draining the whipped cream, all that drips through can be re-whipped.

CHARLOTTE RUSSE.

Cut stale sponge cake into slices about half an inch thick and line three molds with them, leaving a space of half an inch between each slice; set the molds where they will not be disturbed until the filling is ready. Take a deep tin pan and fill about one-third full of either snow or pounded ice and into this set another pan that will hold at least four quarts. Into a deep bowl or pail (a whip churn is better) put one and a half pints of cream (if the cream is very thick take one pint of cream and a half pint of milk); whip it to a froth and when the bowl is full, skim the froth into the pan which is standing on the ice and repeat this until the cream is all froth; then with a spoon draw the froth to one side and you will find that some of the cream has gone back to milk; turn this into the bowl again and whip as before; when the cream is all whipped, stir into it two-thirds of a cup of powdered sugar, one teaspoonful of vanilla and half of a box of gelatine, which has been soaked in cold water enough to cover it for one hour and then put in boiling water enough to dissolve it (about half a cup); stir from the bottom of the pan until it begins to grow stiff; fill the molds and set them on ice in the pan for one hour, or until they are sent to the table. When ready to dish them, loosen lightly at the sides and turn out on a flat dish. Have the cream ice cold when you begin to whip it; and it is a good plan to put a lump of ice into the cream while whipping it.

Maria Parloa.

ANOTHER CHARLOTTE RUSSE.

Two tablespoonfuls of gelatine soaked in a little cold milk two hours, two coffeecupfuls of rich cream, one teacupful of milk. Whip the cream stiff in a large bowl or dish; set on ice. Boil the milk and pour gradually over the gelatine until dissolved, then strain; when nearly cold, add the whipped cream, a spoonful at a time. Sweeten with powdered sugar, flavor with extract of vanilla. Line a dish with lady-fingers or sponge cake; pour in cream and set in a cool place to harden. This is about the same recipe as M. Parloa's, but is not as explicit in detail.

PLAIN CHARLOTTE RUSSE. No. 1.

Make a rule of white sponge cake; bake in narrow shallow pans. Then make a custard of the yolks after this recipe. Wet a saucepan with cold water to prevent the milk that will be scalded in it from burning. Pour out the water and put in a quart of milk, boil and partly cool. Beat up the yolks of six eggs and add three ounces of sugar and a saltspoonful of salt; mix thoroughly and add the lukewarm milk. Stir and pour the custard into a porcelain or double saucepan and stir while on the range until of the consistency of cream; do not allow it to boil, as that would curdle it; strain, and when almost cold add two teaspoonfuls of vanilla. Now, having arranged your cake (cut into inch slices) around the sides and on the bottom of a glass dish, pour over the custard. If you wish a meringue on the top, beat up the whites of four eggs with four tablespoonfuls of sugar; flavor with lemon or vanilla, spread over the top and brown slightly in the oven.

PLAIN CHARLOTTE RUSSE. No. 2.

Put some thin slices of sponge cake in the bottom of a glass sauce dish; pour in wine enough to soak it; beat up the whites of three eggs until very light; add to it three tablespoonfuls of finely powdered sugar, a glass of sweet wine and one pint of thick sweet cream; beat it well and pour over the cake. Set it in a cold place until served.

NAPLE BISCUITS, OR CHARLOTTE RUSSE.

Make a double rule of sponge cake; bake it in round deep patty-pans; when cold cut out the inside about one-quarter of an inch from the edge and bottom, leaving the shell. Replace the inside with a custard made of the yolks of four eggs beaten with a pint of boiling milk, sweetened and flavored; lay on the top of this some jelly or jam; beat the whites of three eggs with three heaping tablespoonfuls of powdered sugar until it will stand in a heap; flavor it a little; place this on the jelly. Set them aside in a cold place until time to serve.

ECONOMICAL CHARLOTTE RUSSE.

Make a quart of nicely flavored mock custard, put it into a large glass fruit dish, which is partly filled with stale cake (of any kind) cut up into small pieces about an inch square, stir it a little, then beat the whites of two or more eggs stiff, sweetened with white sugar; spread over the top, set in a refrigerator to become cold.

Or, to be still more economical: To make the cream, take a pint and a half of milk, set it on the stove to boil; mix together in a bowl the following named articles: large half cup of sugar, one moderately heaped teaspoonful of cornstarch, two tablespoonfuls of grated chocolate one egg, a small half cup of milk and a pinch of salt. Pour into the boiling milk, remove to top of the stove and let simmer a minute or two. When the cream is cold pour over the cake just before setting it on the table. Serve in saucers. If you do not have plenty of eggs you can use all cornstarch, about two heaping teaspoonfuls; but be careful and not get the cream too thick, and have it free from lumps.

The cream should be flavored either with vanilla or lemon extract. Nutmeg might answer.

TIPSY CHARLOTTE.

Take a stale sponge cake, cut the bottom and sides of it, so as to make it stand even in a glass fruit dish; make a few deep gashes through it with a sharp knife, pour over it a pint of good wine, let it stand and soak into the cake. In the meantime, blanch, peel and slice lengthwise half a pound of sweet almonds; stick them all over the top of the cake. Have ready a pint of good boiled custard, well flavored, and pour over the whole. To be dished with a spoon. This is equally as good as any charlotte.

ORANGE CHARLOTTE.

One-third of a box of gelatine, one-third of a cupful of cold water, one-third of a cupful of boiling water and one cup of sugar, the juice of one lemon and one cupful of orange juice and pulp, a little grated orange peel and the whites of four eggs. Soak the gelatine in the cold water one hour. Pour the boiling water over the lemon and orange juice, cover it and let stand half an hour; then add the sugar, let it come to a boil on the fire, stir in the gelatine and when it is thoroughly dissolved, take from the fire. When cool enough, beat into it the four beaten whites of eggs, turn into the mold and set in a cold place to stiffen, first placing pieces of sponge cake all around the mold.

BURNT ALMOND CHARLOTTE.

One cupful of sweet almonds, blanched and chopped fine, half a box of gelatine soaked two hours in half a cupful of cold water; when the gelatine is sufficiently soaked, put three tablespoonfuls of sugar into a saucepan over the fire and stir until it becomes liquid and looks dark; then add the chopped almonds to it and stir two minutes more; turn it out on a platter and set aside to get cool. After they become cool enough break them up in a mortar, put them in a cup and a half of milk, and cook again for ten minutes. Now beat together the yolks of two eggs with a cupful of sugar, and add to the cooking mixture; add also the gelatine; stir until smooth and well dissolved; take from the fire and set in a basin of ice-water and beat it until it begins to thicken; then add to that two quarts of whipped cream, and turn the whole carefully into molds, set away on the ice to become firm. Sponge cake can be placed around the mold or not, as desired.

CHARLOTTE RUSSE, WITH PINEAPPLE.

Peel and cut a pineapple in slices, put the slices into a stewpan with half a pound of fine white sugar, half an ounce of isinglass, or of patent gelatine (which is better), and half a teacupful of water; stew it until it is quite tender, then rub it through a sieve, place it upon ice, and stir it well; when it is upon the point of setting, add a pint of cream well whipped, mix it well and pour it into a mold lined with sponge cake, or prepared in any other way you prefer.

COUNTRY PLUM CHARLOTTE.

Stone a quart of ripe plums; first stew and then sweeten them. Cut slices of bread and butter and lay them in the bottom and around the sides of a large bowl or deep dish. Pour in the plums boiling hot, cover the bowl and set it away to cool gradually. When quite cool, send it to the table and eat it with cream.

VELVET CREAM, WITH STRAWBERRIES.

Dissolve half an ounce of gelatine in a gill of water; add to it half a pint of light sherry, grated lemon peel and the juice of one lemon and five ounces of sugar. Stir over the fire until the sugar is thoroughly dissolved. Then strain and cool. Before it sets beat into it a pint of cream; pour into molds and keep on ice until wanted. Half fill the small molds with fine strawberries, pour the mixture on top, and place on ice until wanted.

CORNSTARCH MERINGUE.

Heat a quart of milk until it boils, add four heaping teaspoonfuls of cornstarch which has previously been dissolved in a little cold milk. Stir constantly while boiling for fifteen minutes. Remove from the fire, and gradually add while hot the yolks of five eggs, beaten together with three-fourths of a cupful of sugar, and flavored with lemon, vanilla or bitter almond. Bake this mixture for fifteen minutes in a well-buttered pudding-dish or until it begins to "set."

Make a meringue of the whites of five eggs, whipped stiff with a half cupful of jelly, and spread evenly over the custard, without removing the same farther than the edge of the oven.

Use currant jelly if vanilla is used in the custard, crab apple for bitter almond and strawberry for lemon. Cover and bake for five minutes, after which take off the lid and brown the meringue a very little. Sift powdered sugar thickly over the top. To be eaten cold.

WASHINGTON PIE.

This recipe is the same as "Boston Cream Pie" (adding half an ounce of butter), which may be found under the head of PASTRY, PIES AND TARTS. In summer time, it is a good plan to bake the pie the day before wanted; then when cool, wrap around it a paper and place it in the ice box so to have it get *very cold*; then serve it with a dish of fresh strawberries or raspberries. A delicious dessert.

CREAM PIE.

Make two cakes as for Washington pie, then take one cup of sweet cream and three tablespoonfuls of white sugar. Beat with egg-beater or fork till it is stiff enough to put on without running off and flavor with vanilla. If you beat it after it is stiff it will come to butter. Put between the cakes and on top.

DESSERT PUFFS.

Puffs for dessert are delicate and nice; take one pint of milk and cream each, the whites of four eggs beaten to a stiff froth, one heaping cupful of sifted flour, one scant cupful of powdered sugar, add a little grated lemon peel and a little salt; beat these all together till very light, bake in gem-pans, sift pulverized sugar over them and eat with sauce flavored with lemon.

PEACH CAKE FOR DESSERT.

Bake three sheets of sponge cake, as for jelly cake; cut nice ripe peaches in thin slices, or chop them; prepare cream by whipping, sweetening and adding flavor of vanilla, if desired; put layers of peaches between the sheets of cake; pour cream over each layer and over the top. To be eaten soon after it is prepared.

FRUIT SHORT-CAKES.

For the recipes of strawberry, peach and other fruit short-cakes, look under the head of BISCUITS, ROLLS AND MUFFINS. They all make a very delicious dessert when served with a pitcher of fresh sweet cream, when obtainable.

SALTED OR ROASTED ALMONDS.

Blanch half a pound of almonds. Put with them a tablespoonful of melted butter and one of salt. Stir them till well mixed, then spread them over a baking-pan and bake fifteen minutes, or till crisp, stirring often. They must be bright yellow-brown when done. They are a fashionable appetizer and should be placed in ornamental dishes at the beginning of dinner, and are used by some in place of olives, which, however, should also be on the table, or some fine pickles may take their place.

ROAST CHESTNUTS.

Peel the raw chestnuts and scald them to remove the inner skin; put them in a frying pan with a little butter and toss them about a few moments; add a sprinkle of salt and a suspicion of cayenne. Serve them after the cheese.

Peanuts may be blanched and roasted the same.

AFTER-DINNER CROUTONS.

These crispy *croutons* answer as a substitute for hard-water crackers and are also relished by most people.

Cut sandwich bread into slices one-quarter of an inch thick; cut each slice into four small triangles; dry them in the oven slowly until they assume a delicate brownish tint, then serve either hot or cold. A nice way to serve them is to spread a paste of part butter and part rich creamy cheese, to which may be added a very little minced parsley.

ORANGE FLOAT.

To make orange float, take one quart of water, the juice and pulp of two lemons, one coffeecupful of sugar. When boiling hot, add four tablespoonfuls of cornstarch. Let it boil fifteen minutes, stirring all the time. When cold, pour it over four or five oranges that have been sliced into a glass dish and over the top spread the beaten whites of three eggs, sweetened and flavored with vanilla. A nice dessert.

LEMON TOAST.

This dessert can be made very conveniently without much preparation.

Take the yolks of six eggs, beat them well and add three cupfuls of sweet milk; take baker's bread, not too stale, and cut into slices; dip them into the milk and eggs and lay the slices into a spider, with sufficient melted butter, hot, to fry a delicate brown. Take the whites of the six eggs and beat them to a froth, adding a large cupful of white sugar; add the juice of two lemons, heating well and adding two cupfuls of boiling water. Serve over the toast as a sauce and you will find it a very delicious dish.

SWEET OMELET. No. 1.

One tablespoonful of butter, two of sugar, one cupful of milk, four eggs. Let the milk come to a boil. Beat the flour and butter together; add to them gradually the boiling milk and cook eight minutes; stirring often; beat the sugar and the yolks of the eggs together; add to the cooked mixture and set away to cool. When cool, beat the whites of the eggs to a stiff froth and add to the mixture. Bake in a buttered pudding-dish for twenty minutes in a moderate oven. Serve *immediately* with creamy sauce.

SWEET OMELET. No. 2.

Four eggs, two tablespoonfuls of sugar, a pinch of salt, half a teaspoonful of vanilla extract, one cupful of whipped cream. Beat the whites of the eggs to a stiff froth and gradually beat the flavoring and sugar into them. When well beaten add the yolks and, lastly, the whipped cream. Have a dish holding about one quart slightly buttered. Pour the mixture into this and bake just twelve minutes. Serve the moment it is taken from the oven.

SALAD OF MIXED FRUITS.

Put in the centre of a dish a pineapple properly pared, cored and sliced, yet retaining as near as practicable its original shape. Peel, quarter and remove the seeds from four sweet oranges; arrange them in a border around the pineapple. Select four fine bananas, peel and cut into slices lengthwise; arrange these zigzag-fence fashion around the border of the dish. In the V-shaped spaces around the dish put tiny mounds of grapes of mixed colors. When complete, the dish should look very appetizing. To half a pint of clear sugar syrup add half an ounce of good brandy, pour over the fruit and serve.

ORANGE COCOANUT SALAD.

Peel and slice a dozen oranges, grate a cocoanut and slice a pineapple. Put alternate layers of each until the dish is full. Then pour over them sweetened wine. Served with small cakes.

When oranges are served whole, they should be peeled and prettily arranged in a fruit dish. A small knife is best for this purpose. Break the skin from the stem into six or eight even parts, peel each section down half way, and tuck the point in next to the orange.

CRYSTALLIZED FRUIT.

Pick out the finest of any kind of fruit, leave on their stalks, beat the whites of three eggs to a stiff froth, lay the fruit in the beaten egg with the stalks upward, drain them and beat the part that drips off again; select them out, one by one and dip them into a cup of finely powdered sugar; cover a pan with a sheet of fine paper, place the fruit inside of it, and put it in an oven that is cooling; when the icing on the fruit becomes firm, pile them on a dish and set them in a cool place. For this purpose, oranges or lemons should be carefully pared, and all the white inner skin removed that is possible, to prevent bitterness; then cut either in thin horizontal slices if lemons, or in quarters if oranges. For cherries, strawberries, currants, etc., choose the largest and finest, leaving stems out. Peaches should be pared and cut in halves and sweet juicy pears may be treated in the same way, or look nicely when pared, leaving on the stems and iced. Pineapples should be cut in thin slices and these again divided into quarters.

PEACHES AND CREAM.

Pare and slice the peaches just before sending to table. Cover the glass dish containing them to exclude the air as much as possible, as they soon change color. Do not sugar them in the dish—they then become preserves, not fresh fruit. Pass the powdered sugar and cream with them.

SNOW PYRAMID.

Beat to a stiff foam the whites of half a dozen eggs, add a small teacupful of currant jelly and whip all together again. Fill half full of cream as many saucers as you have guests, dropping in the centre of each saucer a tablespoonful of the beaten eggs and jelly in the shape of a pyramid.

JELLY FRITTERS.

Make a batter of three eggs, a pint of milk and a pint bowl of wheat flour or more, beat it light; put a tablespoonful of lard or beef fat in a frying or omelet pan, add a saltspoonful of salt, making it boiling hot, put in the batter by the large spoonful, not too close; when one side is a delicate brown, turn the other; when done, take them on to a dish with a d'oyley over it; put a dessertspoonful of firm jelly or jam on each and serve. A very nice dessert.

STEWED APPLES. No. 1.

Take a dozen green tart apples, core and slice them, put into a saucepan with just enough water to cover them, cover the saucepan closely, and stew the apples until they are tender and clear; then take them out, put them into a deep dish and cover them; add to the juice in the saucepan a cupful of loaf sugar for every twelve apples, and boil it half an hour, adding to the syrup a pinch of mace and a dozen whole cloves just ten minutes before taking from the fire; pour scalding hot over the apples and set them in a cold place; eat ice cold with cream or boiled custard.

STEWED APPLES. No. 2.

Apples cooked in the following way look very pretty on a tea-table and are appreciated by the palate. Select firm round greenings, pare neatly and cut in halves; place in a shallow stewpan with sufficient boiling water to cover them and a cup of sugar to every six apples. Each half should cook on the bottom of the pan and be removed from the others so as not to injure its shape. Stew slowly until the pieces are very tender; remove to a glass dish carefully, boil the syrup a half hour longer, pour it over the apples and eat cold. A few pieces of lemon boiled in the syrup add to the flavor.

BAKED PEARS.

Pare and core the pears without dividing; place them in a pan and fill up the orifice with brown sugar; add a little water and let them bake until perfectly tender. Nice with sweet cream or boiled custard.

STEWED PEARS.

Stewed pears with a thick syrup make a fine dessert dish accompanied with cake.

Peel and cut them in halves, leaving the stems on and scoop out the cores. Put them into a saucepan, placing them close together, with the stems uppermost. Pour over sufficient water, a cup of sugar, a few whole cloves and some sticks of cinnamon, a tablespoonful of lemon juice. Cover the stewpan closely, to stew gently till the fruit is done, which will depend on the quality of the fruit. Then take out the fruit carefully and arrange it on a dish for serving. Boil down the syrup until quite thick; strain it and allow it to cool enough to set it; then pour it over the fruit.

The juice could be colored by a few drops of liquid cochineal, or a few slices of beets, while boiling. A teaspoonful of brandy adds much to the flavor. Serve with cream or boiled custard.

BAKED QUINCES.

Take ripe quinces, pare and quarter them, cut out the seeds; then stew them in clear water until a straw will pierce them; put into a baking dish with half a cupful of loaf sugar to every eight quinces; pour over them the liquor in which they were boiled, cover closely and bake in the oven one hour; then take out the quinces and put them into a covered dish; return the syrup to the saucepan and boil twenty minutes; then pour over the quinces and set them away to cool.

GOOSEBERRY FOOL.

Stew a quart of ripe gooseberries in just enough water to cover them; when soft, rub them through a colander to remove the skins and seeds; while hot stir into them a tablespoonful of melted butter and a cupful of sugar. Beat the yolks of three eggs and add that; whip all together until light. Fill a large glass fruit dish and spread on the top the beaten whites mixed with three tablespoonfuls of sugar. Apples or any tart fruit is nice made in this manner.

MERINGUES OR KISSES.

A coffeecupful of fine white sugar, the whites of six eggs; whisk the whites of the eggs to a stiff froth and with a wooden spoon stir in *quickly* the pounded sugar; and have some boards put in the oven thick enough to prevent the bottom of the meringues from acquiring too much color. Cut some strips of paper about two inches wide; place this paper on the board and drop a tablespoonful at a time of the mixture on the paper, taking care to let all the meringues be the same size. In dropping it from the spoon, give the mixture the form of an egg and keep the meringues about two inches apart from each other on the paper. Strew over them some sifted sugar and bake in a moderate oven for half an hour. As soon as they begin to color, remove them from the oven; take each slip of paper by the two ends and turn it gently on the table and with a small spoon take out the soft part of each meringue. Spread some clean paper on the board, turn the meringues upside down and put them into the oven to harden and brown on the other side. When required for table, fill them with whipped cream, flavored with liquor or vanilla and sweeten with pounded sugar. Join two of the meringues together and pile them high in the dish. To vary their appearance, finely chopped almonds or currants may be strewn over them before the sugar is sprinkled over; and they may be garnished with any bright-colored preserve. Great expedition is necessary in making this sweet dish, as, if the meringues are not put into the oven as soon as the sugar and eggs are mixed, the former melts and the mixture would run on the paper instead of keeping its egg-shape. The sweeter the meringues are made the crisper will they be; but if there is not sufficient sugar mixed with them, they will most likely be tough. They are sometimes colored with cochineal; and if kept well-covered in a dry place, will remain good for a month or six weeks.

JELLY KISSES.

Kisses, to be served for dessert at a large dinner, with other suitable confectionery, may be varied in this way: Having made the kisses, heap them in the shape of half an egg, placed upon stiff letter paper lining the bottom of a thick baking pan; put them in a moderate oven until the outside is a little hardened; then take one off carefully, take out the soft inside with the handle of a spoon, and put it back with the mixture, to make more; then lay the shell down. Take another and prepare it likewise; fill the shells with currant jelly or jam; join two together, cementing them with some of the mixture; so continue until you have enough. Make kisses, cocoanut drops, and such like, the day before they are wanted.

This recipe will make a fair-sized cake basket full. It adds much to their beauty when served up to tint half of them pale pink, then unite white and pink. Serve on a high glass dish.

COCOANUT MACAROONS.

Make a "kiss" mixture, add to it the white meat, grated, and finish as directed for KISSES.

ALMOND MACAROONS.

Half a pound of sweet almonds, a coffeecupful of white sugar, the whites of two eggs; blanch the almonds and pound them to a paste; add to them the sugar and the beaten whites of eggs; work the whole together with the back of a spoon, then roll the mixture in your hands in balls about the size of a nutmeg, dust sugar over the top, lay them on a sheet of paper at least an inch apart. Bake in a cool oven a light brown.

CHOCOLATE MACAROONS.

Put three ounces of plain chocolate in a pan and melt on a slow fire; then work it to a thick paste with one pound of powdered sugar and the whites of three eggs; roll the mixture down to the thickness of about one-quarter of an inch; cut it in small, round pieces with a paste-cutter, either plain or scalloped; butter a pan slightly, and dust it with flour and sugar in equal quantities; place in it the pieces of paste or mixture, and bake in a hot but not too quick oven.

LEMON JELLY. No. 1.

Wash and prepare four calf's feet, place them in four quarts of water, and let them simmer gently five hours. At the expiration of this time take them out and pour the liquid into a vessel to cool; there should be nearly a quart. When cold, remove every particle of fat, replace the jelly into the preserving-kettle, and add one pound of loaf sugar, the rind and juice of two lemons; when the sugar has dissolved, beat two eggs with their shells in one gill of water, which pour into the kettle and boil five minutes, or until perfectly clear; then add one gill of Madeira wine and strain through a flannel bag into any form you like.

LEMON JELLY. No. 2.

To a package of gelatine add a pint of cold water, the juice of four lemons and the rind of one; let it stand one hour, then add one pint of boiling water, a pinch of cinnamon, three cups of sugar; let it all come to a boil; strain through a napkin into molds, set away to get cold. Nice poured over sliced bananas and oranges.

WINE JELLY.

One package of gelatine, one cupful of cold water soaked together two hours; add to this three cupfuls of sugar, the juice of three lemons and the grated rind of one. Now pour over this a quart of boiling water and stir until dissolved, then add a pint of sherry wine. Strain through a napkin, turn into molds dipped in cold water and place in the ice box for several hours.

One good way to mold this jelly is to pour some of it into the mold, harden it a little, put in a layer of strawberries or raspberries, or any fresh fruit in season, pour in jelly to set them; after they have set, another layer of jelly, then another of berries, and so fill each mold, alternating with jelly and berries.

CIDER JELLY.

This can be made the same, by substituting clear, sweet cider in place of the wine.

ORANGE JELLY.

Orange jelly is a great delicacy and not expensive. To make a large dish, get six oranges, two lemons, a two-ounce package of gelatine. Put the gelatine to soak in a pint of water, squeeze the orange juice into a bowl, also the lemon juice, and grate one of the lemon skins in with it. Put about two cupfuls of sugar with the gelatine, then stir in the orange juice, and pour over all three pints of boiling water, stirring constantly. When the gelatine is entirely dissolved, strain through a napkin into molds or bowls wet with cold water, and set aside to harden. In three or four hours it will be ready for use and will last several days.

VARIEGATED JELLY.

After dividing a box of Cox's gelatine into halves, put each half into a bowl with half a cupful of cold water. Put three-quarters of an ounce or six sheets of pink gelatine into a third bowl containing three-fourths of a cupful of cold water. Cover the bowls to keep out the dust and set them away for two hours. At the end of that time, add a pint of boiling water, a cupful of sugar, half a pint of wine, and the juice of lemon to the pink gelatine, and, after stirring till the gelatine is dissolved, strain the liquid through a napkin. Treat one of the other portions of the gelatine in the same way. Beat together the yolks of four eggs and half a cupful of sugar, and, after adding this mixture to the third portion of gelatine, stir the new mixture into a pint and a third of boiling milk, contained in a double boiler. Stir on the fire for three minutes, then strain through a fine sieve, and flavor with a teaspoonful of vanilla extract. Place in a deep pan two molds, each holding about three pints, and surround them with ice and water. Pour into these molds, in equal parts, the wine jelly which was made with the clear gelatine, and set it away to harden. When it has become set, pour in the pink gelatine, which should have been set away in a place not cold enough to make it harden. After it has been transferred and has become hard, pour into the molds the mixture of eggs, sugar and gelatine, which should be in a liquid state. Set the molds in an ice chest for three or four hours. At serving time, dip them into tepid water to loosen the contents, and gently turn the jelly out upon flat dishes.

The clear jelly may be made first and poured into molds, then the pink jelly and finally the egg jelly.

STRAWBERRY JELLY.

Strawberries, pounded sugar; to every pint of juice allow half a package of Cox's gelatine.

Pick the strawberries, put them into a pan, squeeze them well with a wooden spoon, add sufficient pounded sugar to sweeten them nicely, and let them remain for one hour that the juice may be extracted; then add half a pint of water to every pint of juice. Strain the strawberry juice and water through a napkin; measure it and to every pint allow half a package of Cox's gelatine dissolved in a teacupful of water. Mix this with the juice, put the jelly into a mold and set the mold on ice. A little lemon juice added to the strawberry juice improves the flavor of the jelly, if the fruit is very ripe; but it must be well strained before it is put with the other ingredients, or it will make the jelly muddy. Delicious and beautiful.

RECIPE FOR CHEESE CUSTARD.

For three persons, two ounces of grated parmesan cheese; the whites of three eggs beaten to a stiff froth, a little pepper, salt and cayenne, a little milk or cream to mix; bake for a quarter of an hour.